POSITIVE FEEDBACK ECONOMIES

Positive Feedback Economies

Elettra Agliardi

Associate Professor of Mathematical Economics, University of Bologna, and Fellow in Economics, Churchill College, Cambridge

First published in Great Britain 1998 by
MACMILLAN PRESS LTD
Houndmills, Basingstoke, Hampshire RG21 6XS and London
Companies and representatives throughout the world

A catalogue record for this book is available from the British Library.

ISBN 0–333–62128–X

First published in the United States of America 1998 by
ST. MARTIN'S PRESS, INC.,
Scholarly and Reference Division,
175 Fifth Avenue, New York, N.Y. 10010

ISBN 0–312–21248–8

Library of Congress Cataloging-in-Publication Data
Agliardi, E. (Elettra)
Positive feedback economies / Elettra Agliardi.
p. cm.
Includes bibliographical references and index.
ISBN 0–312–21248–8 (cloth)
1. Statics and dynamics (Social sciences)   2. Uncertainty.
3. Externalities (Economics)   I. Title.
HB145.A35 1998
300—dc21   97–38691
                                                       CIP

Contents

List of Figures and Tables

Figures

Tables

Preface

This book grew out of research on dynamical economic systems and path-dependence during the preparation of my Ph.D. dissertation, *Essays on the Dynamics of Allocation under Increasing Returns to Adoption and Path-Dependence*, under the supervision of Professor Frank Hahn at the University of Cambridge.

A host of afterthoughts have completely modified the original approach. In preparing this book I have benefited greatly from discussions with numerous colleagues and friends at the Faculty of Economics and Politics, at the Statistical Laboratory, at the Isaac Newton Institute of Mathematical Sciences, at King's College (Workshop on Path-Dependence in Economic Theory) in Cambridge. I am most indebted to Frank Hahn who provided an inspiring mixture of criticism and encouragement in my research over these years and to Partha Dasgupta whose initial guidance led me to study this topic. It is also a pleasant duty to thank the 'Quakers', especially Luca Anderlini, Jayasri Dutta, Robert Evans and Hamid Sabourian, who gave comments and advice on several occasions. This work has also benefited from helpful conversations with Beth Allen, Kalyan Chatterjee, Frank Kelly, David Kendall, Stephen Morris, Ram Ramaswamy, Wolfgang Weidlich and Peter Whittle. Special thanks go to Mark Bebbington and Emanuele Giovannetti who helped me in the simulations of Chapters 4 and 6 respectively.

I also benefited from my stay at Stanford University in 1992, which was very stimulating and fruitful for my research. In particular, I am most grateful to Paul David for enlightening discussions. The contents of this book were presented on several occasions in seminars and workshops: I am also grateful to the participants for their appreciation and their valuable comments.

And finally, I owe a great debt to many friends and colleagues, Fellows at Churchill College. The cultural environment of Churchill College has been a true incentive to my research and has stimulated my interest in an interdisciplinary approach. Without the splendid opportunity of staying at Churchill College, this book could not have been written.

ELETTRA AGLIARDI

Introduction

The objective of this book is to study the economy as a complex system and to show that the presence of self-reinforcing mechanisms in very different economic problems gives rise to common regularities and common qualitative properties. Over recent years the field of complex systems theory has mushroomed. There has been an explosion of research activity within the general area of non-linear sciences, including chaos theory, interacting particle systems, self-organized criticality models, cellular automata theory, simulated annealing learning models, stochastic approximation theory, and many others. Order, disorder, self-organization, synergetics are now notions which constitute parts of the knowledge which is increasingly being transferred from one discipline to another.

We believe that these theories and models describing complex phenomena have the potential of contributing to the understanding of important regularities in economic systems. By 'understanding' we mean here the enterprise of theorizing in economics, and not of being able to make predictions. It is the attempt to gain 'understanding of the particular by reference to generalizing insights and in the light of certain abstract unifying principles' (Hahn, 1985). One of our purposes in this book is to investigate such a challenge: our conviction is that the modelling of economic systems can greatly benefit from the new perspectives that the study of complex phenomena in non-linear dynamic systems has provided to science. Of course, economics has its own specificities, which must be taken into account in any serious theorizing.

In this book, we study dynamical systems of the self-reinforcing type, that is, systems with local positive feedbacks, which are characterized by a multiplicity of asymptotic states or possible equilibrium outcomes. The crucial point is that within this framework 'history matters' in the sense that the equilibrium outcome is history-dependent. The remarkable consequence is that such a perspective leads us to put forward an equilibrium theory which is strongly affected by the information available to agents, their mode of learning about their economic environment, the process of beliefs formation and the evolution of interactions among agents, which are themselves determined by the

1

particular path followed in the economy. Indeed, the path of history is the outcome of individuals' decisions; in turn, the equilibria of an economy depend on its history. Moreover, there can be many histories and so many equilibria an economy can have. In this sense, as Hahn (1989) states, 'there is something essentially historical in a proper definition of equilibrium and of course in the dynamics itself'. More specifically, 'the history of an economy will have an influence not only on which equilibrium an economy finds itself in (if it does find itself in one), but also on the properties of such an equilibrium' (Hahn, 1989).

Traditionally, economic theory has not considered positive feedbacks. But one can find insights scattered here and there in different areas of economics. It is indeed true that economists have recognized that increasing returns can cause multiple equilibria and possible inefficiency at least since Marshall. Multiplicity of equilibria, non-convexities and inefficiency are dealt with in Arrow and Hahn (1971) and in more recent works on open-ended economies such as arise with overlapping generations, showing that there may be a continuum of equilibria, or on economies that lack a full set of Arrow-securities, where in order to overcome this lack of determinateness of equilibrium the behaviour of an economy which evolves according to some process along which agents learn about their economic environment is studied (see, for example, Woodford, 1989). Self-reinforcement goes under different names, such as increasing returns, cumulative causation, dynamic economies of scale, virtuous and vicious circles, in some contributions which date back to the 1920's and 1930's in various fields of economics, such as international trade theory, regional economics, industrial economics, and later in the 1960's with the uprising of interest in growth theories. For example, Young (1928) emphasized the role of increasing returns and dynamic economies of scale, which has already been noted by Smith, in the expansion of markets for industrial products. Kaldor understood that increasing returns and technological progress are intimately related and introduced the idea of cumulative causation, recognizing in various works that the cause of the unevenness of industrial development is increasing returns, that is, success tends to breed further success and failure also tends to be self-perpetuating. Kaldor also regarded cumulative causation as important in explaining the different industrial development paths of different countries: the idea is that some countries which acquire an initial advantage in industrial production tend to consolidate and increase this advantage at the expense of other countries.

Myrdal (1957) pointed to further mechanisms of cumulative causation and of virtuous and vicious circles and Hirschman (1958) studied very similar effects between industries in the context of development economics. A remarkably similar set of ideas are present in modern theories of international trade (Krugman, 1990); in studies in spatial economics and in economic geography (Krugman, 1996), where a parallel between self-organization in time and self-organization in space is drawn, explaining a theory of endogenous differentiation between an industrialized core and an agricultural periphery and the emergence of polycentric patterns in metropolitan areas; in most papers within endogenous growth theory (see, for example, Lucas (1985), Romer (1986); in studies of development economics, where there is a 'population problem' that is related 'synergistically' to poverty (Dasgupta, 1993).

Most examples of positive feedbacks we discuss in this book deal with cumulative causation in the temporal characteristics of 'knowledge' (or information). Knowledge possesses unusual properties. It has the attribute of a public good so that, given a fixed quantity of knowledge, it is the cost of transmission that should determine how widely it ought to be disseminated; there are strong dynamic economies of scale involved in its production and use, which imply irreversibilities in economic activity and the possibility that small changes in such activity result in large changes in the economy's characteristics, as it veers away more and more from its original trajectory; and finally, the uncertainties involved in its use and production are relevant. These features make knowledge a most appropriate example in discussing positive feedback economies, and this will become clear throughout this book, where we also analyse the relevant literature which deals explicitly with technologies and the production of knowledge.

Our approach in this book is mainly mathematical. Certainly, a mathematical formulation is not always a necessary feature of acceptable theorizing. But we feel it ought to be when dealing with the field of complex systems in economics, in order to avoid flabby hand-wringing and easy generalizations from other disciplines, and to force us to specify rather exactly the basis of any pronouncement in this rather new area in economics. Mathematics plays a crucial role in improving our effort to theorize. And as Hahn (1985) says 'if we were all theorists it just might be a better world'.

1 Self-Reinforcing Mechanisms and Complex Economic Dynamics

1.1. ORDER AND DISORDER: THE ECONOMY AS A SELF-ORGANIZED SYSTEM

There is no general agreement as to what constitutes a *complex system*. The term itself has been used in different contexts: it can signify systems with chaotic dynamics; it can also refer to cellular automata, 'neural' networks, adaptive algorithms, disordered many-body systems, pattern-forming systems and so on. Systems that one often thinks of as complex originated in different areas of science: physics, chemistry, biology, computer science, mathematics, phsychology and economics. These systems share some properties which makes them 'complex'.

One of the properties of a complex system is some kind of non-reducibility, that is, the behaviour of a complex system disappears when we try to reduce the system to a simpler one. An enormous amount of data is needed to describe a complex system at a 'microscopic' level. When we use an analytic approach based on the concept of reducibility, the more we are dealing with a complex system, the more we realize that this approach has its own limitation. For example, linearization of the relevant equations governing some complex economic system may eliminate a chaotic behaviour; the kinds of economic patterns which typically arise in the presence of increasing returns disappear if increasing returns are disallowed. Because of the property of non-reducibility we can distinguish a truly complex system from a merely complicated one.

Complex systems display an unexpected behaviour of the system as a whole; that is, an order or pattern emerges out of the initial fluctuations in the system. This 'emergent behaviour' has long been recognized in condensed matter physics, where ordered systems such as crystals or ferromagnets display collective behaviour that cannot be understood in terms of individual atoms considered separately. In economic systems it is important to evaluate which 'structure' emerges from individual choice and decentralized decision-making in 'network' contexts, and how they operate in propagating the influence of historical events. However, it is not necessary to have strongly interacting particles and complicated systems consisting of many parts to find a surprising behaviour: even a simple deterministic one-dimensional map can display chaotic behaviour; a 'structure' can emerge even from simple economic systems with self-reinforcing mechanisms of the kinds discussed by Arthur (1989), having dynamics that are path-dependent; that is, whose position and motion turns out to be 'sensitive to initial conditions'.

There is unpredictability in many complex systems. In some cases the system's trajectories display extreme sensitivity to initial conditions; similarly, one cannot predict the outcome, that is, the final configuration of a system, because of the existence of many locally stable configurations. In all cases extreme sensitivity to initial or boundary conditions or historical path makes prediction almost impossible; nevertheless, relevant regularities do exist, typical patterns may form. The interplay between order and disorder, regularity and chaos, predictability and unpredictability constitute the most striking features of complex systems. A remarkably good definition of what makes a system 'complex' is provided by Philip Anderson, the Nobel laureate physicist, who may perhaps be regarded as the father of the field: complexity is the science of 'emergence'; that is, it is about how large interacting ensembles exhibit collective behaviour that is very different from anything one might have expected from simply scaling up the behaviour of the individual units.

Economics deals with agents that face and rank alternative actions which impinge upon one another, often in a setting of constrained resources. The resulting time-paths of economic actions are called equilibria or solutions and we are interested in the quantitative and qualitative properties of these equilibria.

Complex behaviours in economic systems typically result from the presence of non-linearities due to increasing returns or self-reinforcing mechanisms that induce multiple possible solutions. There are different sources of *self-reinforcing mechanisms* in economics. An example is provided by learning effects, yielding product improvements or lower costs as their prevalence increases. There are also the self-reinforcing effects of decreasing transaction costs due to coordination and reduced signalling and information processing requirements achieved by expanding the 'network' within which individuals' actions conform to behavioural standards or norms. Benefits to individual agents can also arise from temporal coordination of trading activities among holders of inventories and of the interdependence of expenditure and production decisions. Indeed there are advantages to following what other economic agents are doing because of coordination effects, so that, for example, a technology often offers advantages to keeping up with other adopters of it; that is, to belonging to a 'network' of users. Another example of self-reinforcing mechanisms is increased prevalence of some expectations on the market which may enhance beliefs of further prevalence. If many individuals have formulated beliefs, although naively, about some future variable, then they may take actions which tend to bear out their beliefs: self-perpetuating beliefs and 'self-fulfilling prophecies' about such beliefs may arise and become all-important in determining the final outcome in the economy. Finally, large sunk or fixed costs yield falling unit costs to increased output. In all cases self-reinforcing mechanisms imply that a particular outcome or equilibrium possesses or has accumulated an economic advantage. Thus the dynamics are affected by the resulting local positive feedbacks and the outcome which finally occurs is more likely to persist.

The property that multiple equilibria can occur when self-reinforcing mechanisms are present is a crucial one. Loosely speaking, it comes from the fact that when self-reinforcing mechanisms are not offset by countervailing forces, then local positive feedbacks are present, and these can cause amplifications in the deviations of the system from certain equilibria, implying that these equilibria are unstable. For a wide class of economic systems it has been shown that the existence of unstable equilibria implies that there are other equilibria that are stable. Thus the economic system will end up with the equilibria that are stable or attractors. It is important to examine and track how one particular equilibrium is selected from a multiplicity of alternatives; that is, how a particular 'structure' emerges within the economic system and therefore in what way such a system becomes a *self-organized* one. Usually the economic literature that admits self-reinforcing mechanisms studies attractors that are point attractors; in this book, however, we are interested in analysing richer possibilities too.

We shall be mainly concerned with complex economic systems that are self-organized. A system is self-organized if 'it acquires a spatial, temporal or functional structure without specific interference from the outside' (Haken, 1988). Starting from the notion of self-organization within economic systems one can analyze the birth, functioning and decline of market institutions. For example, a system can evolve and originate different productive systems, new products, the creation of intermediaries, of new markets. Typically, the *emergence of order* is characterized by the formation of norms, rules of behaviour among agents, and regularities in the form of conventions and institutions. On the contrary, the evolution of the structures through their transformation and dissolution through chaos determines the *emergence of disorder*. Such analyses require us to take into account the role of 'history' and how this affects the sequence of economic choices and actions. The way in which all this occurs will be made apparent in this book.

1.2. UNCERTAINTY, IRREVERSIBILITY AND INCREASING RETURNS

Self-organization is a dynamic process within a temporal perspective where individuals have to make choices. For a decision problem to be truly dynamic there must be some uncertainty regarding the decision environment, and further this uncertainty must diminish over time. Indeed if there is no uncertainty all decisions could be modelled at the beginning of the decision sequence, while if there is uncertainty the decision-maker takes some action, then receives some new information relevant to subsequent choices and so on, yielding a truly sequential process of decision-making.

The theory of investment decisions of firms has recognized the importance of uncertainty and irreversibility. Most investment expenditures are largely irreversible; that is, they are mostly sunk costs that cannot be recovered. Usually it is the fact that the capital is firm – or industry – specific; that is, it cannot be used productively by a different firm or in a different industry, which makes a cost 'sunk'. When a firm makes an irreversible investment expenditure it gives up the possibility of waiting for new information to arrive that might affect the desirability or timing of the expenditure and cannot disinvest should market conditions change adversely. Put in another way, when considering investment decisions under uncertainty, the irreversibility of investment is significant in as much as it restricts the investor's ability to react to future changes in the decision environment. The presence of irreversible investment expenditure explains the prevalence of *hysteresis*; that is, effects that persist after the causes that brought them about have disappeared. In such contexts, firms may prefer flexible decisions in the early stages of the decision sequence in order to be able to react more easily to new information. As an emerging literature has shown (see, for example, Dixit, 1992a, 1992b; Pindyck, 1991; Dixit and Pindyck, 1994) the ability to delay an irreversible investment expenditure can profoundly affect the decision to invest. In this approach, irreversible investment opportunities are seen as a financial call option. Flexible choices are therefore attractive not because they are safe stores of value, but because they are good stores of options. As a consequence, flexibility as opposed to irreversible commitment can be seen not only as a response to anticipated information but also as a reponse to a different kind of expectation, namely the expectation that new opportunities will arise in the future. A question which still remains unsolved is how to conceptualize future enlargements of the opportunity set and, for example, how to model the production set when uncertainty over future innovations comes into the analysis.

Another important feature of many investment projects is indivisibility. In the presence of indivisibilities there are discontinuities in the choice of investment: if the decision is to invest or not to invest, an individual can immediately cease to invest because of indivisibilities. Individuals in a group may react differently and show qualitatively different behaviour, for example, some of them will invest and others will cease to invest. However, in the presence of uncertainty indivisibilities may be important for investment collapse: if agents base their beliefs on the observation of the others' decision more than on their private information, then 'herd behaviour' may prevail and agents will not invest simply because they base their beliefs on the failure of other agents to invest. There is an analogue of the 'informational cascades' of Bikhchandani, Hirshleifer and Welch (1992) which results in a discontinuity in the choice of investment (Chamley and Gale (1994)).

Prigogine and Stengers (1988) give a list of minimal properties of a system to be a self-organized one: (1) complexity; (2) uncertainty; (3) irreversibility. These are essential ingredients of the economic systems we are interested in.

Most of the examples in this book deal with the dynamics of allocation when there is competition between technologies or technological standards with increasing returns occasioned by learning effects (learning-by-doing and learning-by-using phenomena) or coordination effects (network externalities).

Let us give here a brief definition of such phenomena. Learning-by-doing and learning-by-using are qualitatively different. Learning-by-doing is a phenomenon due to which cost of production decreases with accumulated knowledge, which is usually measured by the volume of production. Another way of defining learning-by-doing, which is less frequent in the literature, is in terms of the effects of cumulated investment on current costs (Arrow, 1962, Sheshinski, 1967). Given a certain volume of production, cost of production also decreases the more a technology is used and the more it is learned about it; that is, the technology improves because of learning-by-using (Rosenberg, 1976). Learning effects involve a form of sunk cost and knowledge is the asset whose cost is sunk. This observation comes from the properties of knowledge, which make it a special commodity: unlike most commodities it decays if it is unused and grows with use; the more it is used, the more durable it is, that is, the less likely it is that it will be forgotten. A piece of knowledge does not need to be produced more than once, it can be used over and over by as many people as wish to at any scale of operation. Thus, the production of knowledge is like a fixed cost in the production of goods and services. Moreover, there can be increased efficiency in the 'technology' of learning through the actual process of learning, the so-called learning to learn (Stiglitz, 1987). The presence of such learning possibilities implies not only an intertemporal externality, but also dynamic economies of scale in production activities. Learning therefore manifests itself as an irreversibility in production possibilities. As a result, if a given firm enjoys some initial advantage over its rival (in terms of initial skills, knowledge, or other forms of sunk costs) it can capitalize on this advantage in such a way that that advantage accumulates over time and makes the rival incapable of offering effective competition in the long run. Accumulation of experience can itself be used as a preemptive move on the part of a firm to deter rivals from entering an industry or, in other circumstances, to make it less and less profitable for rivals to remain in an industry. Put in another way, learning effects may be used for the creation of barriers to entry or to discourage rivals from remaining in the market (Agliardi, 1992b).

Markets exhibit 'network effects' or 'network externalities' when the value of the membership to one user is positively affected when another user joins and enlarges the network. This occurs, for example, in the case of products that are strongly complementary, which are characterized by the fact that they have little or no value in isolation but generate value when combined with others. In many cases the components purchased for a system are spread over time, which implies that buyers must form expectations about availability, price and quality of the components they will be buying in the future. Once a certain system is chosen switching suppliers is costly because new relation-specific investments have to be made. In this situation, systems that are expected to be more popular will be more popular exactly for the reason that this is expected. Of course, such systems pose challenges for coordination among firms and the sort of coordination required by systems competition is often extensive and explicit, including common ownership of various components suppliers, long-term contracts and industry-wide standard-setting bodies.

Learning-by-doing, learning-by-using phenomena and coordination effects in the form of network externalities determine *increasing returns to adoption*, because the more a technology or a technological standard is used and the larger the number of adopters, the larger the benefits from adoption. When increasing returns to adoption are present, 'history matters' in the sense that the equilibrium outcome is history-dependent: the resulting equilibria cannot be understood without knowing the pattern of adoption in earlier periods. When competing technologies possess increasing returns to adoption the following properties, which have been listed and discussed in a series of works by Arthur (1988a, 1988b, 1994), are likely to arise:

- *Multiple equilibria.* If self-reinforcement is not offset by counter-vailing forces, local positive feedbacks are present and, as we said in section 1.1, multiple equilibria can occur. In the case of competing technologies this implies that quite different asymptotic market-share solutions are possible so that the outcome is indeterminate and unpredictable.
- *Lock-in.* This means that once a solution is reached it is difficult to exit from. The dynamics of allocation become structurally rigid and are characterized by the property of inflexibility.
- *Possible inefficiency.* The eventual outcome may not be of maximum possible benefit when a technology has 'bad luck' in gaining early adopters, and yet is 'superior' to another, in the sense that its discounted value of the expected net benefits is higher. In this

case, we say that the market may be locked-in to the 'wrong' technology.

- *Path-dependence*. The dynamics are affected by 'initial conditions', so that the early history of market shares can determine which solution prevails.
- *Symmetry-breaking*. In the case of competing technologies it means that the market starts out symmetric and yet it ends up asymmetric.

Economic theory has long maintained that increasing returns can cause multiple equilibria and possible inefficiency. In this book we shall concentrate on the less familiar properties of lock-in, path-dependence and symmetry-breaking.

1.3. RANDOM ECONOMIES WITH MANY INTERACTING AGENTS

The dynamic evolution of aggregate behaviour resulting from individual interaction is an important element in understanding self-organization in economic systems. Individuals may be influenced by each other's choices, expectations, or simply interact with certain agents. Interactions may be deterministic or stochastic, as may the underlying communication network itself. There can thus be a deterministic set of links used in a random way or the links can themselves be stochastic. In any case, interaction among agents may result in quite complicated dynamics. In some circumstances there is convergence to some solution which remains unchanged over time. In other circumstances the distribution or state at any time changes continually over time and the appropriate equilibrium notion is some limit distribution of the process itself. The difference between the two rests on different structures of the underlying models.

The types of models developed by Arthur (1994) and David (1985, 1987) to explain the adoption of new technologies under increasing returns display, path-dependent dynamics so that the position and motion of the economic system is sensitive to initial conditions, and the stochastic processes studied in those models are 'strongly historical' (David, 1988a, 1988b) in the sense that there is path-dependence of the system's eventual equilibrium outcome. We shall discuss this approach more carefully in Chapter 5. Here we can say, in a concise way, that such systems are usually characterized by: (1) a source of local positive feedback that will systematically reinforce the actions of the agents in the economic system; (2) some source of fluctuations or perturbations independent of the systematic positive feedback effect; (3) something causing the progressive diminution in comparative strength of (2) with respect to (1). If (1), (2), (3) are present, then the resulting path-dependent process is likely to become inextricably 'locked-in'. Indeed, within these models one specific sense of 'history mattering' is the occurrence of lock-in determined by early historical accidents. Without being able to foretell precisely where or just when the system will become 'locked-in' by historical events, it is nevertheless possible to discover that it is bound eventually to end up at one or another among a set of specified equilibrium values. Moreover, in this framework one can also analyze the possibility of sub-optimal outcomes.

These models display the above-mentioned properties of multiplicity of equilibria, path-dependence, lock-in, possible inefficiency and symmetry-breaking. The mathematical tools which are usually applied are a particular class of dynamic resource allocation theories; that is, models of stochastic systems that are characterized by positive feedbacks and possess a multiplicity of locally stable equilibria, or 'absorbing states', and among them the best known is the generalized Polya urn scheme, which was introduced to economists by Arthur, Ermoliev and Kaniovski (1983, 1985). (We shall present the formal structure of this model and the main theorems in Chapter 2, section 2.7). Essentially, the dynamics described in such a model are driven by the continuous growth of a population, the members of which have to make their choices sequentially in an order that is random with respect to their preferences among the set of available alternatives. This scheme is particularly suited for situations where agents decide only once, and irreversibly, and as we said is quite illuminating in characterizing the evolution of market shares and the possibility of sub-optimal outcomes.

There is another class of path-dependent systems which does not display perfect lock-in. These are models which allow 'recontracting' within the market once it has formed. The sense of 'history mattering' is path-dependence of transition probabilities. These models assume an already formed market divided among a certain number of categories. Transitions of units between categories are possible, with probabilities that depend in general on the market shares or number in each category, inducing self-reinforcement. The important difference from the previous models is that with 'deaths' as well as 'births' of adoption allowed, increments to market-share position would tend to be of a constant order of magnitude. As a result, these processes show convergence in distribution rather than strong convergence to a point.

The dynamics in these models are driven by the process of revision of choices within a finite population. Therefore such models allow us to study the evolution of the share held by each technology or standard in a finite adopter population, focusing on the revision and reassessment policies of the adopters. Such revision policies can be directly influenced by positive feedbacks from the 'macrostate' of the system, or may be limited to considering only the actions of the members of a particular reference group, so that in this case positive feedbacks have a locally bounded nature. A set of analytical tools different from those we discussed above are called for. For example, within this approach a particular kind of self-organization we shall be concerned with is the so-called non-equilibrium phase transition: when a system undergoes a transition, the same individuals in the system may give rise to quite different 'macroscopic' states and new qualitative behaviour may emerge. (We shall present some modern techniques and mathematical models suited to this approach in Chapter 2, sections 2.4, 2.5, 2.6.) Loosely speaking, these models are concerned with the features of an adoption process made up of interlinked local structures, where the share of each technology or standard varies on account of choice revisions made by agents and not because of the arrival of new agents. Despite the recurrent reassessment of choices the global process of sequential decisions will display the properties of non-reversibility.

There are various economic applications of models within this category. A few of them consider financial markets and deal with the diffusion of information when there are two competing rumours, beliefs, or opinions, and involve 'herd' or 'epidemic' behaviour, such as those we discuss in Chapter 6, where there is some externality generated by the choices of the other agents in the population. For example, Kirman (1991) considers the case of a market for financial assets where high volatility is obtained if each agent is assumed to actually gain by acting with the majority. Agents' observations include a signal concerning which opinion is held by the majority and observing the behaviour of the majority provides additional information over that obtained by direct encounters. In this model, the diffusion of information is envisioned as a process which includes random factors and which depends on a social network. The social network represents the structure of contacts or the reference groups of individuals, some of whom may be more influential than others, while the randomness can arise from variations in receptivity to the particular information, willingness to experiment or chance encounters with informed individuals. We shall discuss 'recontracting' processes in the context of the choice of technologies with network externalities in Chapter 4 and similar classes of models with other economic applications in Chapter 6.

1.4. THE COEVOLUTION OF TECHNOLOGIES, CONVENTIONS, ORGANIZATIONS AND INSTITUTIONS

A convention is defined as a 'regularity in behaviour which is agreed to by all members of a society and which specifies behaviour in the specific recurrent situation' (Schotter, 1981). A general definition of institutions is less obvious. In abstract terms, institutions can be defined as orderly and more or less persistent behaviour patterns, 'rules or set of rules that constrain or govern organized patterns of behaviours' (North, 1990). These patterns may emerge spontaneously, that is unintentionally, or may result from consciously designed rules of interactions. Some of the institutions are explicitly agreed to and codified into law; others are only tacitly agreed to and evolve endogenously from the attempts of agents to maximize their objective functions. In some cases they supplement markets, in others they totally replace them. Social conventions and the more consciously formalized rules that govern the functioning of organizations and institutions, including many legal institutions, are 'carriers of history' (David, 1994), in the sense that they have evolved into their present forms from similar structures that existed before to satisfy some once important social purpose. On the other hand, because 'institutions are the carriers of history, history must matter in the functioning of market and non-market economies' (David, 1994).

Much of the analysis of how institutions emerge and change over time has been developed within a large class of games, namely coordination and common interest games. We shall consider this class of games again in Chapter 6. The idea is that social norms and institutions are devices that give structure or order to social situations. They do this by giving agents in a particular situation the information about what type of behaviour they can expect from each other. If a certain behavioural regularity appears to become a commonly expected outcome from interactions, then agents may want to account for those expectations provided others do so. Strategic interaction is obviously present, together with a role for 'history': historical experience in the formation of consistent expectations allowing for coordination among agents becomes an important element, and through the reinforcement of mutual expectations 'accidents of history' may acquire a status of durability in social arrangements. This class of games is characterized by a multiplicity of equilibrium points. In the presence of multiple equilibria the question of where the system eventually winds up turns out to be closely related to the study of path-dependence. Moreover, an additional and important question concerns institutional change; that is, the process of replacement of institutions by new ones. This issue is related to the analysis of lock-in phenomena to particular institutions and the possibility of exit from lock-in, an issue to which is attributed a prominent role not only in institutional but also in technological change. Actually, a very similar logic – increasing returns to adoption, or, more generally, a frequency dependence effect – is present when competing technologies or rival institutions are considered. As in the case of competing technologies, the question of which of rival institutions will eventually prevail has to be discussed in terms of strategic interactions.

However, although evolutionary change is now taken by all concerned to be an obvious attribute of institutions, the understanding of the precise workings of the evolutionary process is still at an early stage. For example, one approach in the literature has modelled conventions and institutions as the product of evolutionary processes in which agents are randomly matched with one another and play a particular game. In some cases a deterministic rule is introduced which maps proportions of players using a strategy at time t into proportions at time $t+1$ to define a 'replicator' dynamics and study the basins of attraction of the dynamic process. Stochastic elements are often introduced in the form of 'mutations' that allow strategies to reappear (Foster and Young, 1990; Kandori, Mailath and Rob, 1993). Alternatively, another approach takes into account the experience and information of the agents and allows agents to adjust their strategies individually (Samuelson, 1993; Young, 1993). It will become clear later in this book that although evolutionary game theory has certainly been fruitful for the problem of equilibrium selection, it does not seem to be entirely satisfactory when applied to the study of the evolution of markets and institutions. Institutions can indeed persist for a long period and are even less adaptable than technologies because of stronger complementarities (institutional inertia), but they can collapse more dramatically, either being taken over or abandoned by other institutions. Arnold (1992) has made a first attempt to model an institutional 'catastrophe', using the theory of catastrophes. David (1994) has suggested the theory of 'punctuated equilibria' (Gould and Eldredge, 1972) to capture the idea that the course of change of organizations and institutions is for the most part 'incremental' and almost imperceptible, but suddenly rapid events of 'speciation' and abrupt replacements may arise. Notice however that such theory, although quite fascinating, has not yet received an appropriate mathematical support. Certainly, more sophisticated dynamics are called for to interpret evolutionary change and institutions, and much work still remains to be done in this field.

Some interesting insights about the role of history come from studies of economic anthropologists and economic historians (Boyd and Richerson, 1993; Greif, 1994; North, 1990) who have long conjectured that cultural variations account for intersociety differences in societal organizations. They stress the importance of specific cultural elements – 'cultural beliefs' – in being an integral part of institutions and in affecting the evolution and persistence of diverse societal organizations. For example, different cultural beliefs may imply different social patterns of economic interactions, each of which entails different dynamics of wealth distribution. They may also imply different relations between efficiency and profitability in intrasociety and intersociety economic interactions. Some cultural beliefs can render efficient intersociety relations unprofitable, leading to an economically inefficient social structure. The idea is that past cultural beliefs provide focal points and coordinate expectations, thereby influencing equilibrium selection and society's enforcement institutions. Once a specific organization is introduced it influences the rules of historically subsequent games and hence the resulting societal organization. Thus 'the capacity of societal organization to change is a function of history, since institutions are combined of organizations and cultural beliefs, (. . .) and past organizations and cultural beliefs influence historically subsequent games, organizations and equilibria' (Greif, 1994).

Finally, a further way in which 'history matters' in the evolution of organizations and institutions has to do with the fact that organizations are able to acquire more information than individual economic agents. It has been stressed by Arrow (1974) that information has to be filtered, coordinated and transmitted, and this can be done by acts of irreversible investments, learning indeed, which becomes 'an irreversible capital accumulation for the organization', giving rise to hysteresis in organizational capabilities and institutions. Much can be gained in the study of the evolution of organizations and institutions by analyzing the process of information and the diffusion of knowledge, magnified by interrelatedness and complementarities among distinct institutional arrangements. For this analysis the study of the interactions between institutions and technologies can be of some help. For example, in the case of network externalities property rights may help to solve informational externalities and investment problems. Network ownership is most effective in overcoming network externalities, and even if ownership over some networks may not be possible, many network effects might be internalized by the direct interaction of participants, in the form of particular transactions, contracts, communication systems; at the same time, network sponsors have to make commitments and a way to do it is through vertical integration, building a reputation, sunk investment. The self-reinforcing interactions between property rights and technology may help to explain the diversity of the institutions of production. Moreover, institutional shocks may originate different self-reinforcing relations between property rights and technology and generate new self-sustaining ownership systems. When one accepts this view about the coevolution of technologies, organizations and institutions a great deal of debate in terms of new policy issues is bound to open.

1.5. THE CONTENT OF THE BOOK

In this book we consider the economy as a complex system. We study dynamic systems of the self-reinforcing type; that is, systems with local positive feedbacks, often combined with random elements, having a multiplicity of asymptotic states or possible 'emergent structures'. As we said above, these systems have also been called 'self-organized' systems.

Because the field is quite new and not many people are familiar with it, in order to increase the ease of reading, but also to provide the mathematical apparatus for the proper treatment of this subject, we present and discuss, in an elementary but rigorous way, some mathematical tools which are extensively used in the literature on positive feedbacks and which will be developed in the other chapters of this book. Important elements of differentiable dynamical systems, bifurcation theory, topological dynamics, catastrophe theory, ergodic theory and very recent techniques, such as percolation theory and the theory of self-organized criticality, are presented, and some ways in which these tools can be particularly relevant for economic applications are indicated. Most of these mathematical tools have been developed and traditionally applied in disciplines different from economics. As Nicolis and Prigogine (1989) have recognized 'breaking the disciplinary barriers and trying new ways of looking at sometimes long-standing problems is one of the essential goals of the methods of analysis of complex phenomena.' Certainly, economics has its own specificities and therefore the possibility of an easy generalization should in no way be encouraged. Still, in many cases the modelling of economic systems can strongly benefit from the new perspective that the study of complex phenomena in non-linear dynamic systems has provided to science. Our conviction is indeed that evolutionary theories and complex dynamics are bound to play an increasingly important role in our effort to understand economic systems.

The concepts of irreversibility and increasing returns, the role of uncertainty, the properties of lock-in, path-dependence and symmetry-breaking are extensively discussed in Chapters 3, 4 and 5, where we study, as an application, the choice between technologies or technological standards competing for adoption and the dynamics of allocation under increasing returns to adoption. The kind of increasing returns to adoption we consider in Chapters 3 and 4 are network externalities, while in Chapter 5 we deal with learning effects. The focus of Chapter 3, which examines 'bandwagon effects' in the presence of network externalities, is on the equilibrium adoption path of technological standards. In particular, we show that if network externalities are sufficiently strong, then interesting discontinuities may arise, which can be explained by catastrophe theory. In Chapter 4 we study under what conditions it is possible for an economic system to exit from lock-in. We consider the problem of technological switching in the presence of network externalities, and discuss it within a class of models allowing 'recontracting' in the market, once it has already formed. This chapter also introduces to the economic literature some approximation techniques to solve the resulting stochastic model and to characterize the probability distribution of the proportion of agents adopting the same decision. In Chapter 5 we discuss the properties of multiple equilibria, possible inefficiency, lock-in, path-dependence and symmetry-breaking, following the approach which uses generalized Polya urn schemes to model the role of history when increasing returns to adoption are present. We then study under what circumstances one technology can achieve a monopoly and eventually take the whole market by formulating a firm's optimal decision problem, when both uncertainty and increasing returns to adoption are present, using a more appropriate tool within the theory of statistical decisions, which allows us to strengthen some of the results of the literature about lock-in with competing technologies.

In Chapter 6 we consider also other models, not necessarily about technological choice, dealing with the evolution of the aggregate behaviour resulting from individual interactions in an environment characterized by positive feedbacks. The basic idea underlying the approach in this chapter is that by taking explicit account of the interactions between individual agents we may get interesting regularities at the aggregate level. In particular, this allows us to study the emergence of a variety of rules of thumb, norms, conventions, and institutions. We study dynamic models of local interactions, evolution in games, and models of 'herd behaviour', where there is some externality generated by the choices made by members of the population. Moreover, we introduce the model of self-organized criticality to study the morphogenesis of an institution. By incorporating how agents interact in our models, we not only make them more realistic but also enrich the types of aggregate behaviour that can occur. For this reason, we think that the sort of work discussed in this chapter may represent a further step in the direction of thinking of the economy as a self-organized system. A few final remarks conclude the book.

2 Some Mathematics for Complex Economic Systems

2.1. DYNAMICAL SYSTEMS

The term 'dynamical system' describes a system that evolves in time according to a well-defined rule. More mathematically, a dynamical system is characterized by the fact that the future values of its observable variables can be given as a function of the values of the variables at the present time. The space Σ where such variables are defined is called the *phase space*. The behaviour of dynamical systems is represented in a multidimensional phase space, where the state of the system at any time is represented by a point. The dynamical system describes the change in the states with time; that is, a transformation acting on Σ is given and is called a *flow*. More specifically, associated with each $t \in \mathbb{R}$ (or $t \in \mathbb{R}^+$) there is a mapping $f^t : \Sigma \to \Sigma$ such that the group property holds (that is, $f^0 = Id(\Sigma)$ and $f^{t+s} = f^t . f^s$ for all t, s). The system moves from the state $x \in \Sigma$ to the state $f^t x$ after time t. A *cascade* differs from a flow in that the maps f^t are defined only for integer t. The evolution of a system starting from a given initial state – that is, from a given point x in the phase space – is represented by a *trajectory* in this space; that is, the trajectory of x is the set $\{f^t x\}$. If $t > 0$ we use the prefix semi- for flows, trajectories, etc. If $f^t x = x$ for all t, then x is an *equilibrium point*. If $f^{t+T} x = f^t x$ for all t and for some $T \neq 0$, then the trajectory $\{f^t x\}$ is said to be periodic. Periodic trajectories are closed and are often called cycles. If a set $A \subset \Sigma$ is such that $f^t A = A$ for all t, then A is said to be an *invariant set*.

One of the central questions studied in dynamical systems is *long-time behaviour*. In some dynamical systems (called dissipative dynamic systems) special features of particular initial motions damp out, allowing the system to approach asymptotically – that is, as $t \to \infty$ – a restricted region of phase space (typically of lower dimension than the original phase space) called an *attractor*. More precisely, a closed invariant set A is called an attractor if (1) for every neighbourhood U

21

of *A* there is a neighbourhood *U'* of *A* such that any positive semi-trajectory which starts in *U'* is entirely contained in *U*; (ii) if *x* is sufficiently close to *A* then the distance of *f¹x* from *A* tends to 0 as *t* → +∞. As the name suggests, various initial conditions can be 'attracted': the set of points that are so attracted is called the *basin of attraction*. A dynamical system can have more than one attractor, each with its own basin of attraction. When such multiple basins of attraction exist, different initial conditions lead to different types of long-time behaviour and the boundaries between the basins of attraction become important objects to study.

The simplest attractor in dynamical systems is a fixed point in phase space. For such fixed-point attractors the motion eventually stops: the system is attracted to one point and stays there. For linear dissipative systems fixed points are the only possible attractors. Non-linear dynamical systems, however, have many more possibilities. For instance, their asymptotic behaviour may settle on a time-dependent oscillating state. If the oscillations are represented by a closed curve in the phase space, such periodic attractors are called limit cycles. A standard reference in the economics literature is Goodwin (see Goodwin, 1982) for a collection of the relevant essays), who put forward the idea of illustrating persistent, deterministic oscillations within a multiplier–accelerator setup by means of a limit cycle for a non-linear two-dimensional dynamical system.

For dynamical systems evolving in phase space of dimension greater than two the repertoire of behaviours becomes amazing: there can be periodic attractors (cycles of order *k*), quasi-periodic attractors (invariant tori), non-periodic attractors, chaos and strange attractors – so named precisely because of their bizarre and unanticipated properties. Motion on a strange attractor exhibits most of the properties associated with randomness, although the equations of motion are fully deterministic and no explicit randomness is added: the 'random' behaviour arises intrinsically from the non-linear dynamical systems and the structure of its attractor. Although over short times it is possible to follow the trajectory of each initial point accurately, over longer periods tiny differences in the original position are greatly amplified so that detailed predictions of the asymptotic behaviour become impossible.

Figure 2.1 shows some examples of attractors: (a) cycles of order *k*; (b) invariant tori; (c) three examples of chaotic attractors (they have been found by Edward N. Lorenz, by Otto E. Rössler and by Robert S.

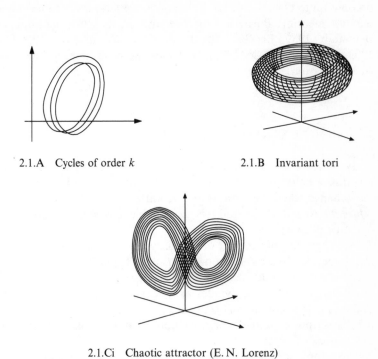

2.1.A   Cycles of order *k*   2.1.B   Invariant tori

2.1.Ci   Chaotic attractor (E. N. Lorenz)

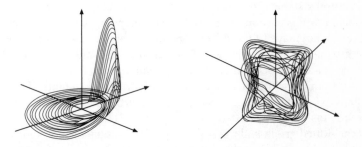

2.1.Cii   Chaotic attractor (O. E. Rössler) 2.1.Ciii   Chaotic attractor (R. S. Shaw)

Figure 2.1   Examples of attractors

Shaw, respectively). More recently the study of chaotic behaviour has become quite fashionable in the economics literature (among others, we can mention Barnett, Gewerke and Shell, 1989; Baumol and Benhabib, 1989; Brock, 1990; Boldrin and Woodford, 1990; Day, 1993; Medio and Gallo, 1992). Our book, however, does not deal with such behaviour.

2.2. BIFURCATIONS

A dynamic system may depend on one or more real parameters. The qualitative behaviour of the system, that is the nature of its attractors, may change when the parameters are varied. Such changes are called *bifurcations* and their study is a valuable guide in understanding dynamic phenomena.

More specifically, let $(f_u{}^t)$ denote a dynamical system depending on a parameter u (the bifurcation parameter). Typically, u will be a real variable but it could also be a collection of such variables. If the qualitative nature of the dynamical system changes for a value u_0 of u, one says that a bifurcation occurs at u_0. In particular, we are interested in a description of the reorganizations that take place as u passes through u_0.

The bifurcation notion may be formalized by introducing the concept of *structural stability*. Let D be a specific space of differentiable dynamical systems and call the set of points described from a given point, when t varies, the orbit of a point. A point (f^t) of D is said to be structurally stable if for every (g^t) sufficiently near (f^t) in D, there is a homeomorphism (that is, a continuous mapping with a continuous inverse) that maps (f^t)-orbits to (g^t)-orbits, preserving the order of the points on the orbits. The set of points in D that are not structurally stable is a closed set and is called the *bifurcation set*.

An example will explain the concept of structural stability. The map $f(x) = x^2$ is stable since if we push (perturb) the graph of the map slightly (as shown by dotted lines in Figure 2.2) the topological pictures of the dotted graph and the solid graph are the same. More rigorously, the dotted curve is just the graph of a reparametrization of f. So what we wish to do is to characterize maps that are stable. They are nice in the sense that when we perturb them a little we can still predict their topological type. The natural question is whether there are enough

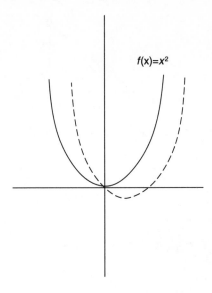

$f(x)=x^2$

Figure 2.2   Structural stability

stable maps. In other words, can any map be approximated by a stable map? This is a typical question about *genericity*. To define genericity properly we have to introduce the notion of a residual set; that is, the set of D which contains a countable intersection of dense open subsets of D. If a property of dynamic systems is true in a residual subset of D, this property is said to be generic.

Typically, we are interested in generic bifurcations. Examples of generic bifurcations are the flip bifurcation and the Hopf bifurcation, whose diagrams are depicted in Figure 2.3a and 2.3b. In the flip bifurcation a family of periodic orbits of period 2 is created when u increases beyond u_0. In the Hopf bifurcation a family of invariant circles appears when u increases beyond u_0. For a complete mathematical analysis of generic bifurcations the interested reader can refer to Guckenheimer and Holmes (1983); interesting economic applications are developed, for example, in Benhabib and Nishimura (1979), Cugno and Montrucchio (1983), and Grandmont (1987).

If a stable equilibrium state describes the conditions in some real system, say in economics, then when it merges with an unstable

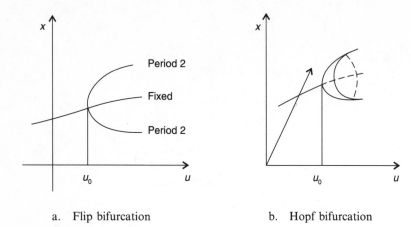

a.   Flip bifurcation   b.   Hopf bifurcation

Figure 2.3   Examples of bifurcations

equilibrium state the system must jump to a completely different state: as the parameter is changed the equilibrium condition in the neighbourhood considered suddenly disappears. It was jumps of this kind which lead to the term 'catastrophe theory'.

2.3.   CATASTROPHIC BEHAVIOUR

A great many of physical, social, economic phenomena involve discontinuities. There are systems whose behaviour is usually smooth, but which sometimes exhibits discontinuities or, in other words, there are sudden changes caused by smooth alterations. Catastrophe theory, developed by the mathematician René Thom, provides a technical tool which captures a broad range of such phenomena. In this section we illustrate some basic themes of this theory.

Suppose that the state of a system at any time can be completely specified by the values of n variables $(x_1, \ldots, x_n)$ – state or internal variables – which are determined (though not quite uniquely) by m variables $(u_1, \ldots, u_m)$ – control or external variables – thus the phase space is $n + m$ dimensional. A typical example to which the theory applies is a system with gradient dynamics, that is $\dot{x} = -\mathrm{grad}\, V_u(x)$.

The state of the system is found at one of the minima of V_u, because these are precisely the attractors of $-\text{grad } V_u(x)$. If the state lies at a minimum of V_u which is destroyed through perturbation of u, the system will experience a catastrophic change as the state is directed to a new minimum.

Thus, roughly speaking, a catastrophe is an abrupt change in the number of minima possessed by functions in a family as the parameters defining the family vary continuously. What catastrophe theory tells us is that the number of 'qualitatively' different configurations of discontinuities that can arise depends on the number of control variables, and if this number is small there are only a few distinct types of catastrophes whose properties have been completely described. It is thus possible to predict much of the qualitative behaviour of the system even if the number n of the state variables is very large, and without carrying out a detailed analysis of the equations governing the system.

Let us illustrate the rise of a catastrophic behaviour through an example. Assume that the control factors are two conflicting factors, say u and v, and let x denote the state variable. Let G denote a likelihood distribution for x, whose maxima represent the most likely state, and suppose that G has the graph in Figure 2.4. Note that in the last case (Figure 2.4.d) the distribution has gone bimodal. We can plot the most likely behaviour above the control-space (u, v), as it is done in Figure 2.5. Note that for large v and small u the surface M is 2-sheeted and $v = \text{constant}$ intersects M in a disconnected graph. When a boundary point of this graph is reached, there is a sudden jump onto

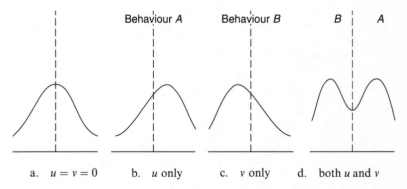

	Behaviour *A*	Behaviour *B*	*B* *A*
a. $u = v = 0$	b. *u* only	c. *v* only	d. both *u* and *v*

Figure 2.4   Catastrophic behaviour

the upper (or the lower) sheet. The curve on the surface where the upper and the lower sheets fold over into the middle sheet is called the fold-curve, and its projection on the horizontal plane is called the bifurcation set. Here the bifurcation set has a sharp point, forming a cusp (cusp-catastrophe). The cusp lines form the thresholds for sudden behavioural change. When a point of this line is reached there is a sudden jump up (down) onto the other sheet.

The most characteristic properties of the cusp catastrophe are: *sudden jumps, divergence, bimodality, inaccessibility, hysteresis.* By divergence we mean that slight differences in the path may (without any jumps) produce large differences in state, even when they start and end at the same control point (see Figure 2.6): all that matters is that the two paths pass on either side of the cusp point. By bimodality we mean that for certain points there are two possible stable states (see Figure 2.5). Inaccessibility means that if a point is above or below the bimodality region, we can give the state variable any value we like, by moving the control variables, but if the point is level with the bimodality region

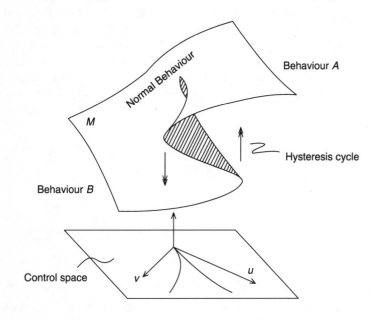

Figure 2.5   Sudden behavioural change

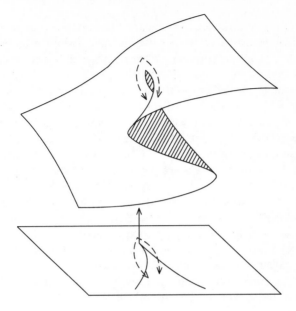

Figure 2.6   Divergence

there are certain values of the state variable (for example 0) at which stable equilibrium is not possible. Finally, hysteresis means that if we reverse the path in the controls, we do not necessarily reverse the path in the state space. If we move the control variables back and forth across the bimodality region, the jumps to the right do not occur at the same place as the jumps to the left (see Figure 2.5). This is a more technical way of defining irreversibility.

2.3.1.   Classification of Catastrophes

Let us now provide a more rigorous classification of catastrophes. For this purpose we need some more mathematics, so the reader who is not properly equipped may skip this subsection. We say that a function undergoes catastrophe when it is embedded in a family in such a way that the number of minima possessed by neighbouring functions is not constant. If a function f has only non-degenerate critical points (that

Positive Feedback Economies

is, the Hessian matrix is non-singular), then any function near f has as many minima as f (see Morse theory), and then f cannot undergo catastrophe. Thus we consider f having a degenerate critical point, and being embedded in a family $F(., u)$, where we assume $F(., 0) = f$. Such an embedding is called an *unfolding*. A catastrophe is individuated by a function f at a degenerate critical point of f (actually, we consider 'germs' of functions, that is we identify all the functions that coincide in some neighborhood of a point, since the cause of catastrophe is local), where the number of minima of the functions in the unfolding varies. The simplest unstable maps are $y = x^3$ and $y = x^4$, and each function sufficiently close to them can be proved to be equivalent to $x^3 - ux$ and $x^4 - ux^2 - vx$ respectively. Consider for example the catastrophe family $F(x, u, v) = x^4 - ux^2 - vx$, whose critical points are non-degenerate, unless (u, v) lies on the cusp-shaped curve $27v^2 - 8u^3 = 0$. Points not on the cusp correspond to non-catastrophic functions. The cusp-curve is called the catastrophe set of $y = x^4$.

More generally, the catastrophe set K of an arbitrary catastrophe consists of those points $u \in \mathbb{R}^m$ for which $F(., u)$ has a degenerate germ which itself can undergo catastrophe.

One basic question in catastrophe theory is the classification of catastrophes. Since we are interested only in qualitative properties of catastrophes, we will consider two catastrophes equivalent (that is, with identical qualitative properties) if one can be obtained from the other by appropriate diffeomorphisms. In order to get information about the structure of a catastrophe set we must introduce *Zeeman's catastrophe manifold M* of an unfolding F, which is $M = \{(x, u) \in \mathbb{R}^n \times \mathbb{R}^m;$ $\text{grad}_x F(x, u) = 0.\}$ Define the catastrophe map $\xi : M \to \mathbb{R}^m$ to be the restriction of the projection $\mathbb{R}^n \times \mathbb{R}^m \to \mathbb{R}^m$ to M. Let us see through an example, the fold, that the singular set of ξ (in M) consists of the degenerate critical points of the unfolding and the projection of the singular set to the control space is the catastrophe set K, that is, K is the apparent contour of ξ. Let $F_u(x) = x^3 - ux$ be an unfolding of $y = x^3$. Then $M = \{(x, u); 3x^2 = u\}$, see Figure 2.7. Now we recall a fundamental theorem in catastrophe theory:

Thom's Theorem

If $m \leq 5$, any singularity of ξ is equivalent to one of a finite number of types called *elementary catastrophes*, and ξ is locally stable at all points

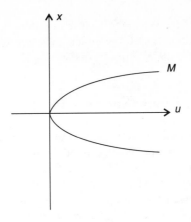

Figure 2.7   The catastrophe manifold

of *M* with respect to small perturbations of *F*. The number of elementary catastrophes (e.c.) depends only on *m*, as follows:

m	1	2	3	4	5	6
e.c.	1	2	5	7	11	∞

The catastrophe maps giving the eleven elementary catastrophes are the following: x^3, x^4, x^5, x^6, x^7, $x^3 + xy^2$, $x^3 - xy^2$, $x^2y + y^4$, $x^3 + y^4$, $x^2y + y^5$, $x^2y - y^5$. Their pet names are the following: fold, cusp, swallowtail, butterfly, wigwam, umbilic catastrophes (hyperbolic, elliptic, parabolic, symbolic, second hyperbolic, second elliptic).

Until now we have recalled only the first two catastrophes, which are the only ones occurring with two control variables and are the most interesting for economic applications: that is, the fold (where the bifurcation set is a single point, and to its left there are two states, one maximum and one minimum, and to its right there are none) and the cusp (the bifurcation set is a cusp-shaped curve). In Chapter 3 we will see an economic interpretation of an elementary catastrophe.

If there are three control variables and one state variable, the swallowtail-catastrophe also appears; with more state variables two more singular points are possible (the hyperbolic and the elliptic umbilic), and so on. We refer to the specialized literature for an analysis of the geometry of the other catastrophes (Zeeman, 1977; Poston and Stewart, 1978; Saunders, 1980; Arnold, 1992).

2.3.2. Beyond Elementary Catastrophe Theory

A few final remarks are in order. One of the advantages of catastrophe theory is that it can be applied also when the data are not quantifiable or when, for example, it is difficult to write down the appropriate differential equations. In catastrophe theory the variables are defined up to diffeomorphisms and all that we need are topological properties, such as proximity, smoothness, increase and decrease. If in a system we recognize divergence, sudden jumps, or hysteresis, we may attempt to fit a catastrophe model to the dynamics of the system. Thus we can expect some qualitative conclusions starting from some qualitative data; this is why catastrophe theory has found successful applications in several fields.

However, elementary catastrophe theory is insufficient in many applications. For instance, there are dynamics that are not gradient-like and consequently there is no function to be minimized. Non-elementary catastrophes can occur (such as the Hopf bifurcation). Thom himself wrote that most systems can only be described by '*generalized catastrophes*'. The essential idea is that an attractor which up to a certain time is governing in a certain domain, then ceases to do so, and is replaced by some new attractors, each governing only part of the domain.

Finally, we can say that complicating a model realistically complicates the behaviour, and elementary catastrophe theory becomes insufficient in the highly structured and organized complexity of an economy or some other system. For example, approximate knowledge of the initial state can be useless for long-time prediction and the system can exhibit chaotic behaviour. In this case more powerful tools are required in the analysis of these complex systems. Thom's view is that singularity theory and the elementary catastrophes are only a small part of catastrophe theory and that all mathematical theories which describe how abrupt changes take place in families of objects depending smoothly on parameters should be included in catastrophe theory. However, such a comprehensive theory has not yet achieved a mathematical completeness.

2.4. SYMMETRY-BREAKING AND BROKEN ERGODICITY

Whereas simple systems typically possess unique stable states, complex systems have many non-equivalent alternatives. The passage toward complexity is intimately related to the bifurcations of new branches of solutions caused by the non-linearities and the constraints acting on a system. Bifurcations sometimes generate solutions displaying *broken symmetries*. This happens whenever starting with dynamics which display 'symmetry' we observe the generation of states each of which is 'less symmetrical' than the dynamic laws themselves.

Let us consider an example. Take $(1/4)x^4 + (u/2)x^2$, whose equation of state is $x^3 + ux = 0$. As an unfolding among even functions of x, that is, those with $f(x) = f(-x)$, we find that $(1/4)x^4 + (u/2)x^2$ is the unique stable single-parameter local family around $x = 0$ up to the usual diffeomorphisms (themselves symmetric under the map $x \rightarrow -x$). Notice that although $(1/4)x^4 + (u/2)x^2$ has the specified symmetry throughout, the individual solutions to the minimization problem for $u < 0$ do not (see Figure 2.8.a and the bifurcation diagram in Figure 2.8.b). Thus a system which adopts one minimum or the other 'breaks' the symmetry. The symmetry is however not lost to the minimization problem because the set of minima still possesses it. We can say that the symmetry of the problem has fragmented into a symmetry of the set of solutions which is held by them only collectively.

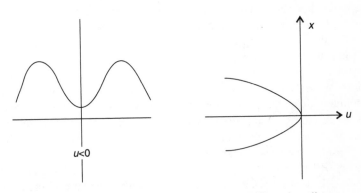

a. Solution to the minimization problem for $u < 0$

b. Bifurcation diagram

Figure 2.8   Broken symmetries

Let us define here the concept of symmetry group in order to give a more general and rigorous definition of 'symmetry-breaking'. We recall that a 'symmetry' is a transformation that leaves an object invariant; that is, it looks the same after applying the symmetry as it did to begin with and it is replaced into the same space that it started from. To express this fact, we say that the symmetries of an object form a group. A group is indeed a closed system of transformations: whenever two of them are combined the result is another member of the same group. We call this particular group the 'symmetry group' of the object. A useful definition that will be used later is that of a representation of a group. A representation of a group G on a vector space W is a homomorphism $T : g \rightarrow T(g)$ of G into the group of invertible linear transformations on W, that is, $T(g_1)T(g_2) = T(g_1g_2)$. Homomorphisms are important because they are exactly the maps from one group to another that preserve group structure. A homomorphism which is 1–1 and onto is said to be an isomorphism. An isomorphism of a group onto itself is called an automorphism, and the set of all automorphisms of a group itself forms a group, the automorphism group. Given a spatial configuration F, those automorphisms of space which leave F unchanged form a group, and this group describes exactly the symmetry possessed by F. This is another way of saying that group theory provides the adequate mathematical language to define symmetry. It also provides the language to define 'symmetry-breaking' adequately, and this can be done by introducing group theory into bifurcation theory. Let us see how.

Suppose that the dynamics of the economic system takes the form $\dot{x} = G(u, x)$, where u is a parameter in Λ, x is an element of a vector space Σ and $G(.)$ is a mapping from $\Lambda x \Sigma$ to a vector space Ψ. Consider an equation of the form $G(u, x) = 0$ in the neighbourhood of a known solution (u_0, x_0). Bifurcations may occur when $G_x(u_0, x_0)$ is not invertible. We define the notion of *bifurcation equations* by applying the Lyapounov–Schmidt procedure, which is a procedure traditionally used for reducing an infinite dimensional problem to a finite dimensional one (see Golubitsky and Schaeffer, 1985). That is, we consider $G(u, x) = 0$, where $G(.)$ is an analytic mapping from $\Lambda x \Sigma$ to Ψ and suppose $G(0, 0) = 0$ and that $L_0 = G_x(0, 0)$ is a particular operator (namely a Fredholm operator of index zero with kernel μ of dimension n). We assume $\Sigma \subset \Psi$ so that the projection P on to the kernel μ maps Σ into Σ and Ψ into Ψ. Let $Q = 1 - P$ be the projection onto the range of L_0 in Ψ. We decompose $G(u, x) = 0$ into the system $QG(u, w + \varphi) = 0$ and $PG(u, w + \varphi) = 0$, where $w = Px$, $\varphi = Qx$. The first equation $QG(u, w + \varphi) = 0$ is solved for $\varphi = \varphi(u, w)$ by the implicit function theorem; $QG(u, w + \varphi) = 0$ has locally a unique solution $\varphi(u, w)$ analytic in u and w. We then substitute this solution in the second equation $PG(u, w + \varphi) = 0$ to obtain the bifurcation equations:

$$F(u, w) = PG(u, w + \varphi(u, w)) = 0$$

Solutions of $F(u, w) = 0$ are locally in one-to-one correspondence with solutions of the system $QG(u, w + \varphi) = 0$ and $PG(u, w + \varphi) = 0$, hence with solutions of the original equation $G(u, x) = 0$ in the neighbourhood of the bifurcation point $(0, 0)$. A basic result concerns the group invariance of the bifurcation equations:

Theorem (Sattinger, 1977; 1978). Let $G(u, x) = 0$ be invariant with respect to a group representation $T(g)$ of some group G. That is, assume that $T(g)G(u, x) = G(u, T(g)x)$, where $T(g)$ is a representation of G on the spaces Σ and Ψ. The bifurcation equations $F(u, w) = 0$ are then invariant with respect to the finite dimensional representation $T(g)$ restricted to the kernel, that is, $T(g)F(u, w) = F(u, T(g)w)$.

From this theorem we can classify bifurcation problems according to the geometry of the problem. Typically, in many economic problems the equations describing the system are invariant under some transformation group. When bifurcation problems arise in such a situation the group invariance may lead to multiplicities of the branch point. Such a multiplicity is a crucial aspect in pattern formulation problems. What the theorem above states is that if the nonlinear equations admit a symmetry group, then, under sufficiently general conditions, this symmetry is inherited by the corresponding bifurcation equations. Ultimately, through the introduction of group theory into bifurcation theory one can classify the possible bifurcating patterns entirely from symmetry considerations and independently of the particular structure of the equations.

The vector solutions, however, may not be invariant under the entire group but only under some subgroup of the original group. For example, the Hamiltonian of an economic system may have some symmetry group G but the behaviour of the system has only the symmetry of a subgroup $G_0 \subset G$; obviously, there are then a set of equivalent possible behaviours corresponding to elements of the coset space G/G_0. Symmetry breaks if the behaviour of the economic system fails to show the symmetry of its underlying Hamiltonian; hence the term 'symmetry-breaking'. When symmetry breaks, the symmetry of the resulting state of the system is a subgroup of the symmetry group of the whole system. So 'symmetry-breaking' is a change in the symmetry group, from a larger one to a smaller one, from the whole to a part. Now we can finally give the following definition:

Definition. Suppose that an economic system possesses a stable solution invariant under a symmetry group G for a given range of a parameter u. We say that 'symmetry-breaking' occurs if as u crosses a critical parameter u_c new solutions appear which are invariant only under a subgroup G_0.

The term *broken ergodicity* was coined to refer to a generalization of broken symmetry. Let us recall here the notion of ergodicity.

Ergodic theory concerns the flow of probability in phase space given some dynamics. Let us call S a subspace of the phase space consistent with any constraints. Under the dynamics each initial point $x_0 \in S$ will lead to a trajectory $x(t)$ on S with $x(0) = x_0$. This flow is said to be *ergodic* if for almost all x_0 the trajectory $x(t)$ passes through every small neighbourhood of S. Given deterministic dynamics $x(t)$ cannot pass through every point of S, but, if ergodic, comes arbitrarily close to any specified point, although it may take a very long time to cover all S. We define the time mean of a quantity X evaluated along the trajectory $x(t)$ to be:

$$\lim_{T \to \infty} [\frac{1}{T} \int_0^T X(x(t)) dt]$$

and the phase or space mean of $X(x)$ as:

$$\frac{1}{\Omega} \int_S X(x) dx$$

where Ω is the volume $\int_S dx$ of S. (2.1) is known as the *Mean Ergodic Theorem*:

$$\lim_{T \to \infty} [\frac{1}{T} \int_0^T X(x(t)) dt] = \frac{1}{\Omega} \int_S X(x) dx \qquad (2.1)$$

This asserts that the time average equals the space average. The so-called *ergodic distribution* can then be determined, namely, the particular stationary distribution which is such that the right side or the left side of (2.1) appear as averages over this distribution of all allowable values of the quantities $X(x)$.

When ergodicity is broken a system does not visit every region of its allowed phase space S on the timescale considered. This means that under *broken ergodicity* a system is confined to some subregion S^α with $S^\alpha \subset S$, and there are typically many possible such subregions. Thus, when a system is non-ergodic the position and motion of the dynamic system is sensitive to initial conditions; the existence of many possible subregions leads naturally to *history-dependence*, including irreversibility, memory and hysteresis.

Broken ergodicity is an ingredient of broken symmetry, but it is more general. In complex systems indeed, one can obtain a significant breakdown of ergodicity in which the different possible subregions, or components, are not symmetry-related; that is, there can be broken ergodicity without, or beyond, broken symmetry.

2.4.1. Phase Transitions

Some examples of broken symmetry and broken ergodicity can be discussed in the context of *phase transition models*. Bifurcation theory and catastrophe theory are necessary components for a rigorous treatment of such models.

A standard example to describe phase transitions comes from ferromagnetism. The Ising ferromagnet is a very simple model of a magnet, in which an array of magnetic ions, or spins, are arranged on a regular crystal lattice and interact both with each other and with an external magnetic field. Above a critical temperature T_c a substance may be paramagnetic; that is, the spins are not coupled to one another, being about half up and half down. But below T_c the system 'breaks the symmetry' and acquires a non-zero magnetization: below T_c there are two branches, one with most of the spins up and one with most of the spins down. The system is not ergodic. Taken together the two possible states do have average magnetization 0 but in fact one finds one state or the other not both at once. Figure 2.9 depicts the probability $\pi(M)$ of finding the system with given magnetization M: for $T > T_c$ there is one maximum at $M = 0$ and for $T < T_c$ there are two maxima,

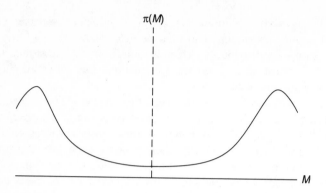

Figure 2.9   The order parameter and broken ergodicity

corresponding to the two branches we discussed above. *M* is called the *order parameter*. It is the parameter that characterizes the broken symmetry for this problem.

This example illustrates how phase transition models can describe a particular kind of self-organization: microscopic elements give rise to quite different macroscopic states, which change abruptly from one state to another. The structure of phase transition models can be considerably simplified if the so-called 'slaving principle' can be applied. The 'slaving principle' which has been elaborated by Haken (1983) sets in if in a dynamic system one can distinguish slow variables and fast variables. The fast variables quickly develop into their momentary equilibrium values, whereas the remaining slow variables do not move substantially during the adaptation time of the fast variables. The momentary equilibrium values of the fast variables can therefore be expressed by the values of the remaining slow variables. That is, they are 'slaved' by the slow variables. After the elimination of the fast variables one obtains a reduced approximate system of equations of motion for the slow variables alone. Thus, the slow variables dominate the dynamics of the system: they are called order parameters.

In many cases of practical interest the number of order parameters may be very small or even one, where the number of 'slaved' variables is still very large. Changes in the order parameter determine changes in the phase of the system. The order parameter has a magnitude that is usually 0 above a critical value and then becomes non-zero below it. In particular, we say that there is a *first-order phase transition* if the order parameter jumps to a finite value, discontinuously, at the critical value, and a *second-order phase transition* if the order parameter grows from 0 continuously below the critical value.

An application of this approach to social sciences is in Weidlich and Haag (1983) and Weidlich (1991). Starting from the decisions of individuals, the central equation of motion, that is, the master equation, is constructed for the probability distribution over the possible macroconfigurations of society. Then, from the master equation they derive the equations of motion for the expected values of the macro-variables of society. Typically, these equations are non-linear and by varying order parameters phase transitions between different modes of social behaviour can be described. Föllmer (1974) has given, albeit extremely stylized, examples of Ising economies. He developed an equilibrium analysis of large exchange economies and showed that if there is strong local random interaction among agents who are *a priori* identical, then one can no longer infer the probability which governs the joint behaviour of all the agents from the microeconomic characteristics of the individuals, and macroeconomic irregularities can arise. In order to specify a particular type of interaction, Föllmer introduced a neighbourhood structure; that is, each agent is only influenced by a finite number of other agents and this structure is defined *a priori*. It is worth noting that Föllmer worked within a static framework, whilst most of the recent work on interaction and inter-dependence has been in the context of dynamic stochastic processes. We shall present an economic application within a dynamic framework in Chapter 4 and discuss related models also in Chapter 6.

2.4.2. Some Models of 'Interacting Particles' Systems

Phase transition models have been particularly successful in the case where a spatial array of variables interact with each others. In order to study local interactions one has effectively to impose some graph-like structure on the phase space. It has been developed by models of interacting 'particles' systems, whose relevance for economics has been extensively discussed in David (1988a, 1988b), David and Foray (1994). Examples of interacting 'particles' systems that are of some interest for economists include: the voter model and the biased voter model; the contact process and epidemic models; percolation, oriented and regular. All these models have a common feature: that is, they have a critical value and have the property that when subcritical the phenomena under study die out exponentially fast and when supercritical they grow linearly and have an asymptotic shape. Accordingly, they exhibit a phase transition.

Let us see how these models work. Denote by $z_t \subset Z^d$ the state at time t, where Z^d is the d-dimensional integer lattice; the points in z_t are typically thought of as being occupied by a 'particle' (agent), so that z_t is the set of 'occupied sites'. Points are added or deleted from z_t at rates that depend upon $n_t(x) =$ number of occupied neighbours, the neighbours of a point in Z^d being the $2d$ points closest to some x. The following rules hold:

$$\text{If } x \notin z_t, \text{ then prob}(x \in z_{t+s}|z_t) = s\alpha(n_t(x)) + o(s)$$
$$\text{If } x \in z_t, \text{ then prob}(x \notin z_{t+s}|z_t) = s\omega(n_t(x)) + o(s)$$

where the birth rate α and death rate ω depend upon the model in question. In the biased voter model $\alpha(n) = \lambda n$ and $\omega(n) = 2d - n$. That is, sites become occupied at a rate equal to λ times the number of occupied neighbours, and become vacant at a rate proportional to the number of vacant neighbours (the voter model is a particular case of the biased voter model where $\lambda = 1$). The reason for the name is apparent if we imagine that each point is occupied by a voter of one of two political parties, and the voter changes his party affiliation at a rate proportional to the number of neighbours in that party. One can show that if $\lambda > 1$ and the system starts with one occupied site, then with probability $(\lambda - 1)/\lambda$, sites do not become vacant, but the number of occupied sites grows linearly and has an asymptotic shape. The interpretation is that eventually the system approaches complete consensus. The contact process is characterized by the same birth rate as the biased voter model, but a death rate $\omega(n) = 1$. It can be used to represent the spread of an epidemic, or information diffusion. Here there is a critical λ, say λ_c, such that if $\lambda > \lambda_c$ the 'infection' has a positive probability of not dying out starting from $z_0 \neq 0$, and if $\lambda < \lambda_c$ the system dies out whenever z_0 is finite, and dies out exponentially fast. In the biased voter model $\lambda_c = 1$. The voter model fits into this picture as the biased voter model at the critical value.

A rigorous treatment of these models is beyond the purpose of this chapter, and so the interested reader can refer to classical references such as Durrett (1988), Kindermann and Snell (1980), Liggett (1985). The comparatively new field in stochastic process analysis referred to as 'percolation theory' is an important technical tool which can be fruitful in the study of positive feedbacks economies. We therefore postpone the discussion of percolation theory to a separate section.

2.5. PERCOLATION THEORY

By the term 'percolation' we refer to the dual of a diffusion process. 'Diffusion' refers to the random movements of particles through an ordered non-random medium, while the term percolation conjures up the image of droplets of water moving under the deterministic pull of gravity through a disordered random medium. When the water entering at some source sites eventually finds its way into enough open channels to pass throughout, we say that complete percolation has occurred – from whence the statistical models of analogous processes take their name. Percolation theory is concerned primarily with the existence of such 'open paths'.

In two dimensions, let Z^2 be the plane square lattice and let p be a number such that $0 \leq p \leq 1$; we examine each edge of Z^2 in turn and interpret p as the probability that an edge is open (and $1 - p$ that it is closed) independently of all other edges. If we delete the closed edges, we are left with a random subgraph of Z^2; what we have to study is the structure of this subgraph, particularly with regard to the way in which this structure depends on the numerical value of p. The resulting process is called a *bond* model, since the random blockages in the lattice are associated with the edges. Another type of percolation process is the *site* model in which the vertices rather than the edges are declared to be open or closed at random. Here we shall consider bond percolation only: although bond percolation is a less general model, it exhibits the majority of properties expected of more general percolation-type models, and is sufficiently simple, incorporating as it does a minimum of statistical dependence.

Let us use some terminology from graph theory to establish the basic definitions and notation of (bond) percolation on Z^d. We may turn Z^d into a graph, called the d-dimensional cubic lattice L^d, by adding edges between all pairs x and y of points of Z^d, with the distance from x to y equal to 1. Let us write Z^d for the set of vertices of L^d. We define a path as an alternating sequence $x_0, e_0, x_1, e_1, \ldots e_{n-1}, x_n$ of distinct vertices x_i and edges $e_i = <x_1, x_{i+1}>$. Such a path has length n and is said to connect x_0 to x_n. Consider the random subgraph of L^d containing the vertex set Z^d and the open edges only. The connected components of this graph are called *open clusters*. We write $C(x)$ for the open cluster containing the vertex x and C for the open cluster at the origin; we denote by $|C(x)|$ the number of vertices in $C(x)$.

A central notion is the *percolation probability* $\theta(p)$, which is the probability that a given vertex belongs to an infinite open cluster. By the translation invariance of the lattice and probability measure, we lose no generality by taking this vertex to be the origin and thus we define:

$$\theta(p) = P_p(|C| = \infty).$$

It is important to percolation theory that there exists a critical value $p_c = p_c(d)$ such that:

$$\theta(p) = \begin{cases} = 0 \text{ if } p < p_c \\ > 0 \text{ if } p > p_c \end{cases} \tag{2.2}$$

where $p_c(d)$ is called the *critical probability* and is defined in the following way: $p_c(d) = \sup[p : \theta(p) = 0]$. In one dimension, if $p < 1$ there are infinitely many closed edges of L^1 to the left and to the right of the origin almost surely, so that $\theta(p) = 0$ if $p < 1$; thus $p_c(1) = 1$. The situation is quite different in two and more dimensions. In two dimensions there is a famous exact calculation theorem, which is considered to be one of the most important milestones in the theory of percolation, stating that $p_c(2) = 1/2$. When $d > 2$ it is highly unlikely that there exists a useful representation of any $p_c(d)$, although non-trivial upper and lower bounds may be found and calculated with increasing degrees of accuracy with the aid of computers. The following theorem (Kesten, 1982) amounts to the statement that there is a non-trivial critical phenomenon in dimensions two and more.

Theorem

If $d \geq 2$ then $0 < p_c(d) < 1$.

That is, there are two phases of the process: a subcritical phase when $p < p_c(d)$ – and all open clusters are almost surely finite – and a supercritical phase when $p > p_c(d)$ – and each vertex has a positive probability of being in an infinite open cluster, so that there exists almost surely at least one infinite open cluster. In this sense, percolation is one of the simplest systems that exhibits a phase transition.

The probability $\theta(p)$ is a non-decreasing function of p. This is intuitively obvious, because an increase in p leads to an increase in the number of open edges of L^d, and therefore increases the number and length of open paths from the origin. There are also other important characters for percolation apart from $\theta(p)$: for example, the mean number of vertices in the open cluster at the origin (that is, the mean size of the open cluster at the origin), or the number of open clusters per vertex. Actually, the basic questions in percolation theory concern both the size and shapes of typical open clusters as the edge-probability p varies from 0 to 1, and large-scale phenomena such as the existence of infinite open clusters.

We have said that when $p < p_c$ all open clusters are almost surely finite, while when $p > p_c$ there exist almost surely infinite open clusters. An important question then becomes the following: how many infinite open clusters will emerge when $p > p_c$? There are theorems stating that the infinite open cluster is almost surely *unique* (see, for example, Grimmett (1989)). The additional question is: what does this cluster look like? The geometry of the infinite cluster, and particularly its properties of statistical self-similarity over different length-scale, are indeed interesting but very little rigorous progress has been made in this direction even in the case of two dimensions. A first step towards understanding the geometry of the infinite cluster in two dimensions is to estimate its density. Kesten (1986) has shown that we may think of the infinite cluster as being a subset of L^2 having a 'fractal dimension'. We recall here that the term 'fractal', which was coined by Mandelbrot, refers to geometrical objects characterized by self-similarity, that is, objects having the same structure on all scale: the whole object can be obtained as the infinite replica of each part of a fractal object. As an example of a natural fractal one can think of a snowflake (see Figure 2.10). The infinite cluster is self-similar in the sense that, if we view this cluster at a lower resolution, then the details will become blurred but it looks similar. The overall structure of the cluster, for instance the fact that there are holes in the cluster at all possible sizes, remains. To be more precise, we say that a set of points is self-similar if it is invariant with respect to translation and scaling. It is useful to consider bounded sets such as a finite piece of a line. A finite line

Figure 2.10   Generation of a snowflake

segment does not have translational symmetry – moving it results in a new set of points. However, if we change lengths by the scale factor r less than one, we generate a new set of points which may be translated to cover a part of the original line. If we choose r properly, we may cover the original line once with N non-overlapping segments. We say that the original set of points is self-similar with respect to the scaling ratio r. In general, we can define the similarity dimension as $D = -\ln N / \ln r(N)$. Grimmett (1989) studied some aspects of the geometry of the infinite open cluster. In particular, he showed that the 'surface' of the infinite cluster has the same order as its volume, that is, the ratio of boundary to volume of the infinite cluster tends to $(1 - p)/p$ if $p_c < p < 1$.

Percolation theory is a comparatively new and unexplored field for economists. David and Foray (1994) suggest an application to the study of the adoption of technological standards when economic agents are embedded in local networks. The model which is suggested is a mixed percolation model, where both vertices and edges can be blocked. Each vertex represents an organization, responsive (open vertex) to the influence of any of its neighbours' standards choices, or unresponsive (closed vertex) to local network externalities in deciding on its standards, while each edge is an inter-organizational transactions line, attaining some minimal or threshold density of transactions between the two adjacent organizations (open edge), or failing to do so (closed edge). An operative path is said to be 'open' in this context if all its transactional links attain the minimum sufficient density and all its organizations are influenced by network externalities in selecting their standard. What can be observed is that the system undergoes a phase transition, because there can be a coexistence of multiple standards, as a manifestation of the sub-criticality of the inter-organizational transactions system, and spontaneous emergence of a unique standard in the region where complete percolation is achieved.

2.6. THE THEORY OF SELF-ORGANIZED CRITICALITY

A related problem to percolation is analysed in the theory of self-organized criticality (SOC). The elegant and bold hypothesis proposed by Per Bak and his colleagues at the Brookhaven National Laboratory in the USA is that many large, multicomponent systems which change over time organize themselves into a special state called *self-organized critical* state. To illustrate the self-organized critical state Bak's group proposed a computer model of a 'sand pile', built from uniform square grains stacked on top of each other in columns. Grains are added to the pile, one at a time, onto the tops of the columns. The locations for the added grains are chosen at random so that the pile grows with an uneven surface. However, when the height difference between neighbouring columns reaches some predetermined threshold the surface grains flow, or fall, from the higher to the lower column. In turn, this movement may leave other neighbouring columns in an unstable condition so that further surface flow could occur. The computer model completes all the surface movements in a chain or *avalanche* process, before any more grains are added.

It is apparent from this model that the ideas that support SOC unify concepts such as self-organization and catastrophe. Even the smallest events happening before the critical state is attained can greatly influence the final configuration, but once the final state is attained, it is relatively difficult to disturb. The critical state can actually be an attractor for the dynamic system, toward which the system naturally evolves, and to which it returns after being perturbed by some external shock. The criticality in this theory is fundamentally different from the critical point at phase transitions, which can be reached only by the tuning of a parameter; here, instead the system evolves to the critical state without detailed specification of the initial conditions, and such critical state is robust with respect to variations of parameters.

Self-organized critical systems have been studied mainly through computer simulations and controlled experiments. They have been applied to the study of earthquakes and forest fires, to volcanic eruption and turbulence, to biological evolution and very recently to economics. Here we shall present the model of SOC formally.

In the Bak, Tang and Wiesenfeld (1988) models of SOC to each site x on a d-dimensional hypercubic lattice is associated an integer variable $z(x)$. The dynamics of the model are discrete, non-linear, and diffusive and defined by the rule that if any $z(x)$ exceeds a critical value z_c, then the variables at m neighbouring sites increase by 1, while $z(x)$ decreases by m. Without loss of generality we choose $z_c = m$ and in the steady state the zs then take the m values $0, 1, 2, \ldots m - 1$. For example, take $z_c = 2$, so that if $z(x) \geq 2$ then $z(x) \to z(x) - 2$. If we start from an arbitrary configuration of all 1s and a particle is added at random sites, we can eventually reach an SOC state which is statistically stationary, and such that subsequent addition of a particle leads to reorganization on all length scales, as it is represented in the matrix below. The system evolves until all zs are less than 2, at which point another particle is added at a random site:

$$
\begin{array}{l}
\ldots 1\ 1\ 1\ 2\ 1\ 1\ 1\ 1 \ldots \\
\ldots 1\ 1\ 2\ 0\ 2\ 1\ 1\ 1 \ldots \\
\ldots 1\ 2\ 0\ 2\ 0\ 2\ 1\ 1 \ldots \\
\ldots 2\ 0\ 2\ 0\ 2\ 0\ 2\ 1 \ldots \\
\ldots \ldots \ldots \ldots \ldots \ldots \ldots
\end{array}
$$

To make things easier we follow Dhar and Ramaswamy (1989), by introducing a preferred direction, say that of the steepest descent (following the sand pile analogy, $z(x)$ is interpreted as the height of a sand column at the point x), and we put $m = d$. We define the longitudinal coordinate of a site $x = (x_1, x_2, \ldots, x_d)$ as $T(x) = \Sigma x_i$ and consider the model in a finite lattice confined to the region $0 \leq T \leq L$. Particles are added at random on the top (that is, at the surface $T = 0$) and drop off the pile at $T = L$. Using the terminology from the sand pile analogy, when $z(x)$ exceeds z_c, that column 'topples' and the effect of a toppling is to create an avalanche. Avalanches are characterized by a duration, which is the number of constant T surfaces affected by the toppling, and by a mass, which is the total number of sites that toppled.

Any configuration satisfying $0 \leq z(x) \leq d - 1$ for all x is a stable configuration. If we denote by S the number of sites on each constant-T surface, the total number of such configurations is d^{LS}. Dhar and Ramaswamy (1989) show that for finite S there is a non-zero probability that all sites on some surface $T = T_0$ will topple. This makes all sites on surface $T_0 + 1$ topple as well and this self-perpetuating state leads to infinite avalanches. If S is infinite, they show that the probability that in the SOC state the avalanche has a duration greater than t varies as $t^{-\alpha}$ for large t, where α is some exponent which can be determined. A striking feature of this model is that when $d = 2$ all sites that topple on a line $T =$ constant must be contiguous, and therefore the cluster of toppled sites in an avalanche has no holes. The boundary of such a cluster is formed by the path of two annihilating random walks, starting at the origin, each taking steps with equal probability, and exhibiting a behaviour that is exactly equivalent to a case of (directed) percolation. The case $d \geq 3$ is presently being investigated by

Ramaswamy (private communication), but what can certainly be said is that the SOC state is not characterized as simply as above and the dynamic rules appear to allow holes in avalanche clusters.

In most experiments and simulations of SOC it has been found that activity exhibits non-trivial power law correlations in both space and time; that is, there is a power law distribution of cluster sizes and time scales. The distribution of cluster sizes is determined by counting the number of affected sizes generated from a perturbation at one site and averaging over many arrays. A distribution of cluster sizes leads to a distribution of fluctuation lifetimes, namely how long the noise propagates after perturbation at a single site, weighted by the temporal average of the response. In order to evaluate the prediction power in a dynamic system both initial conditions and the laws determining evolution have to be known precisely enough. A property of systems displaying SOC is that the uncertainty in the initial conditions increases at a slower rate than in chaotic systems: while in chaotic systems it increases exponentially, in SOC systems a power law can be observed. We say that the systems displaying SOC are weakly chaotic, and that the behaviour of such systems 'adapt to and on the edge of chaos' (Kauffman, 1992).

A very nice application of SOC to economics has been proposed by Bak, Chen, Scheinkman and Woodford (1993). They study the effects on the aggregate economy of many small independent shocks to different sectors of the economy, when significantly non-linear, strongly localized interactions between different parts of the economy exist. The context is an extremely simple model of a large number of firms where each buys goods from, and sells goods to, a small number of neighbouring firms, using the goods they buy to produce the goods they sell. The exogenous shocks that drive the economy are independent fluctuations in the flow of purchases of a large number of different types of final goods. The dynamics are of the following character. Each of the random orders received by a final goods producer initiates a chain reaction whose length depends upon the initial configuration. If the firm receiving the order can fill it out of existing inventories, no further orders are generated. Otherwise, it produces and sends orders to two neighbouring firms, and so on. As a consequence, a cascade of production may arise. The kind of macroscopic instability that can result is then studied with the theory of SOC, and the size of the avalanche of the total production that occurs by all the firms involved can be measured. Other economists have become aware that fluctuations in economics might indeed be 'avalanches' in an SOC state of that system. While traditional models usually assume the existence of a stable equilibrium position for the economy, whereby large aggregate fluctuations can result only from external shocks affecting many different sectors in the same way and simultaneously, the view of the economy as an SOC system allows us to expect more or less periodic large-scale fluctuations, even in the absence of any common jolts across sectors. Benoit Mandelbrot of IBM has analysed indicators such as the Dow Jones index and found fluctuations similar to those predicted in SOC models in financial markets. Stanley and others (1996) have examined corporate growth and organizational infrastructures and recognized the importance of scaling laws to describe the growth of companies. We shall present a model of SOC to discuss the morphogenesis of an institution in Chapter 6.

2.7. PATH-DEPENDENCE AND LONG-TIME BEHAVIOUR: THE ROLE OF 'HISTORY'

Many stochastic processes of the self-organizing type studied by economists and discussed in this book are characterized by non-linearities, positive feedbacks, and as a result, typically possess a multiplicity of possible asymptotic solutions. Instability or sensitivity to initial conditions and perturbations determine which solution or 'structure' will be selected from the multiplicity of alternatives, because the cumulation of early fluctuations pushes the dynamics into the orbit of one of the possible alternatives. These systems are non-ergodic – there are multiple outcomes and early perturbations become relevant in the selection of a 'structure'. These systems are said to be *path-dependent*, because the state at time *t* depends on the states at previous times.

Within this class of stochastic processes it is important to investigate the emergence of a 'structure' by deriving theorems on asymptotic behaviour. The theorems by Arthur, Ermoliev and Kaniovski (AEK) provide an answer to this question, by constituting a generalization of the strong law of large numbers to a wide class of path-dependent stochastic processes. These theorems are mentioned very often in the economics literature about self-reinforcing mechanisms; therefore, in what follows we will recall some of their main results.

Positive Feedback Economies

AEK consider path-dependent processes as generalized urn schemes of the Polya kind. The standard Polya case is as follows. Think of an urn of infinite capacity to which are added balls of two possible colours, say red and black. Start with one red and one black ball in the urn, and add a ball each time, indefinitely, according to the rule: choose a ball in the urn at random and replace it; if it is red, add a red one, if it is black, add a black one. Polya proved in 1931 that a strong law can be found for this process with path-dependent increments, so that the proportion of red (or black) balls settles down to a limit X, and with probability one. The limit X is a random variable uniformly distributed between zero and one. A first generalization of the standard Polya scheme (AEK, 1983, 1985) consists of an urn of infinite capacity with balls of N possible colours, instead of just two, where new units are added at each time with probabilities that are not necessarily equal to, but a function of the proportions. Following the notation of AEK (1985), let the vector $X_n = (X_n^1, X_n^1, \ldots X_n^N)$ describe the proportions of balls of types $1, \ldots N$ at time n, let $b_1 = (b_1^1, b_2^1, \ldots b_1^N,)$ be the initial vector of balls at time 1, with $\gamma = \Sigma_i b_i^i$, and let $\{q_n(x)\}$ be a sequence of vector-functions mapping the proportions of colours into the probabilities of an addition to each colour at time n (so that one ball is added to the urn at each time and at time n it is of colour i with probability $q_n^i(X_n)$, with $\Sigma_n q_n^i(X_n) = 1$). At time n, define the random variable

$$\beta_n^i(x) = \begin{cases} 1 \text{ with probability } q_n^i(x) \\ 0 \text{ with probability } 1 - q_n^i(x), i = 1, \ldots N \end{cases}$$

so that the addition of i-type balls to the urn follows the dynamics

$$b_{n+1}^i = b_n^i + \beta_n^i(X_n), \quad n \geq 1.$$

Dividing through by the total number of balls $(\gamma + n - 1)$, the evolution of the proportion of i-types is described by:

$$X_{n+1}^i = X_n^i + \frac{1}{\gamma + n} [\beta_n^i(X_n) - X_n^i], \text{ with } X_1^i = b_1^i / \gamma$$

which can be written as:

$$X_{n+1}^i = X_n^i + \frac{1}{\gamma + n}[q_n^i(X_n) - X_n^i] + \frac{1}{\gamma + n}v_n^i$$

where $v_n^i = \beta_n^i(X_n) - q_n^i(X_n^i)$ represents the perturbation term. The expected motion of X_{n+1} is directed by the non-linear term $q_n^i(X_n) - X_n^i$ and can be written as:

$$E\{X_{n+1}^i | X_n\} = X_n^i + \frac{1}{\gamma + n}[q_n^i(X_n) - X_n^i].$$

Notice that the standard Polya process discussed earlier is characterized by a vector-function $q(.)$ that is identically equal to x, and so has no expected motion driving it.

The fundamental result here is that if $\{q_n(x)\}$ possesses a limit-function q and the process converges, it converges to a limit which belongs to a subset of the fixed points of q. In particular, among the fixed points only the stable ones are attractors. The following theorems summarize this result:

Theorem (AEK, 1985, p. 291)

Given continuous functions $\{q_n\}$, suppose there exists a Borel function $q : S \rightarrow S$, constants $\{a_n\}$, and a (Lyapunov) function $v : S \rightarrow R$ such that:

(1) $\sup_{x \in S} \| q_n(x) - q(x) \| \leq a_n, \Sigma_{n=1}^{\infty} a_n/n < \infty$.
(2) The set $B = \{x : q(x) = x, x \in S\}$ contains a finite number of connected components.
(3) v is twice differentiable; $v(x) \geq 0$, $x \in S$; $< q(x) - x, v_x(x) > < 0$, $x \in S \backslash U(B)$, where $U(B)$ is an open neighbourhood of B.
   Then $\{x_n\}$ converges to a point of B or to the border of a connected component.

Theorem (AEK, 1985, p. 293)

Let ζ be a stable point in the interior of S. Given a process with transition function $\{q_n\}$ which maps the interior of S into itself and which converges in the sense that $\sup_{x \in U \subset S} \| q_n(x) - q(x) \| \leq a_n$, $\Sigma_{n=1}^{\infty} a_n/n < \infty$ then $\text{prob}\{X_n \rightarrow \zeta\} > 0$.

Moreover, given an additional Hölder condition (that is, $\| q(x) - q(\varphi) \| \leq k \| x - \varphi \|^{\mu}$ for $x \in U$ and for some $k, \mu, \in (0,1)$), it can be established that convergence to unstable points has probability zero. AEK (1985) give also the conditions under which the urn may converge to single-colour dominance; that is conditions under which X_n may converge to a vertex of the simplex S. They simply amount to the following: (a) that the vertex is reachable from the starting point, and (b) that $q^N(x)$ approaches 1 sufficiently fast as X approaches the vertex. Arthur's papers contain economic applications of these theorems, and we shall discuss them in Chapter 5.

These convergence results can be sharpened for separable vector-functions $q(.)$ – we recall that a function q is separable if $q(x) = (q^1(x^1), \quad q^2(x^2), \ldots q^{N-1}(x^{N-1}), \quad q^N(x^N) = 1 - \Sigma_{i=1}^{N-1} q^i(x^i))$ – which satisfy a requirement that the q(.) function does not cross the diagonal 'too often'. More precisely, among the set of points to which the process may converge we call the interior fixed point φ a 'downcrossing point' of the function $q(.)$ if for all indices $i = 1, \ldots N - 1$ in some neighbourhood U of φ we have $x^i < q^i(x^i)$ where $x^i < \varphi^i$, and $x^i > q^i(x^i)$ where $x^i > \varphi^i$. 'Upcrossing points' are defined analogously. Then, in the case of separable q-functions and under the above-mentioned definitions we can state the following results:

Theorem (AEK, 1985, p. 297)

If $q : \text{Int}S \to \text{Int}S$, then the process converges to downcrossing points φ with positive probability.

Theorem (AEK, 1985, p. 298)

Suppose $q(.)$ is continuous and has a single interior fixed point φ which is a point of upcrossing for each index i and where each upcrossing satisfies the above-mentioned Hölder condition. Then the process converges to one of the vertices with probability one.

Figure 2.11 illustrates the theorems for the case $N = 2$, which is an important case included in the class of separable q-functions. In Figure 2.11a there is convergence to a 'downcrossing point', while in Figure 2.11b there is convergence toward 0 or 1.

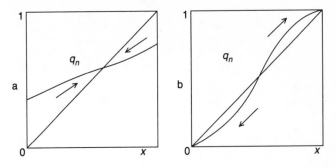

Figure 2.11   Convergence to stable points

More general non-linear Polya processes have been studied in AEK (1987a), where the case of discontinuous q-functions and the case of random additions of balls instead of unit increments at each time are considered. In the last case, which has also been studied by Blum and Brennan (1980), one has to consider an urn of infinite capacity with vector β_n of n colour balls at time n, where $\beta_n(x)$ is a random vector such that $\text{prob}\{\beta_n(x) = i\} = q_n(i, x), \Sigma_i q_i(i, x) = 1$, and the ith coordinate of $\beta_n(x)$ equals the number of i-type balls added to the urn at time n. These generalizations are particularly important for applications in economics (Dosi and Kaniovski, 1993) and for the study of learning in games modeled as Polya urn schemes (Posch, 1993).

3 Network Externalities and Discontinuous Adoption Paths

3.1. BANDWAGON EFFECTS

The possibility that agents may react discontinuously to continuous changes in their environments does not seem to have been sufficiently investigated in economics. Intuition suggests that continuously changing causes should produce continuous effects. However, as we discussed in Chapter 2, catastrophe theory makes clear that the occurrence of discontinuities in smoothly evolving systems is not an unlikely event. One of the purposes of this chapter is to show that 'catastrophes' can arise in a simple model of the adoption of innovations when self-reinforcing mechanisms are introduced.

The kinds of self-reinforcing mechanisms we consider in this chapter are 'network externalities'. We say that there are network externalities when there are benefits from compatibility; that is, when the value of a technological standard to any one user depends on how many others are adopting it, or, in other words, when 'bandwagon effects' are present.

This can occur either in the case of direct physical or communications network externalities; that is, the case where one consumer's value for a good increases when another consumer has a compatible good (as in the case of telephones or personal computer software); or in the case of market-mediated externalities, that is, a complementary good (servicing, software, spare parts, etc.) becomes cheaper and available the greater the extent of the compatible market. The first form of externality operates directly upon the demand side of the market, where the benefits derived by users increase with the number of others whose decision to use compatible products enlarges the coverage of the network. The second form impacts upon the technical performance of a particular system, and feeds back to affect the cost and profits of other component suppliers through the influence of the system's performance characteristics upon users' demand for it in comparison with alternative technologies. The 'hardware/software' paradigm is a good example of network effects which applies to any systems markets: computer hardware and software; credit-card networks (the card is the hardware, merchant acceptance the software); durable equipment and repair services (the equipment is the hardware, the repair the software); the typewriter keyboard (the typewriter is the hardware, experience on that keyboard the software). These hardware/software systems form the sort of virtual networks that give rise to feedback effects similar to those associated with other physical networks.

The subject of network externalities has been much in vogue since the 1980s. In most models (Dybvig and Spatt, 1983; Farrell and Saloner, 1985, 1986a, 1986b; Katz and Shapiro, 1985, 1986a, 1986b; Rohlfs, 1974) the core problem is that markets are likely to work poorly as mechanisms for quickly achieving the degree of compatibility or standardization required to maximize the benefits obtainable with an already existing network technology. The reason for this comes from a sort of public good problem arising when network externalities are present. Early adopters, who help to initiate widespread adoption, risk loss if adoption does not become widespread. Avoiding this risk may induce the following result: either an agent feels obliged to adopt, hoping to start a domino chain, or each agent may wait forever, hoping that other agents will bear the risk of adopting early. Agents who adopt early thereby furnish a public good. A subsidy scheme is suggested by Dybvig and Spatt (1983) in order to get agents to start adopting against the possibility that no or few agents adopt. The work of Rohlfs (1974) on positive externalities in communication networks contains much of the intuition of Dybvig and Spatt (1983), including the idea of equilibrium in terms of the number of adopters and of a domino chain of adopters. The start-up problem is again a question of getting beyond the 'critical mass' and Rohlfs (1974) suggests a policy of a low introductory price to get the 'bandwagon' rolling. Similar kind of inefficiencies arise if there is a status-quo standard, and a new, possibly better, technology appears on the market. Farrell and Saloner (1985, 1986b) show that sometimes the market will not switch even though it should. They call this effect 'excess inertia'. There can be also the opposite phenomenon of wrongly abandoning a technology, which they call 'excess momentum'. These inefficiencies can arise either from problems of coordination and communication or from the importance of the installed base.

A common theme of these approaches is that network externalities likely lead to multiple equilibria, some of which Pareto dominate others. A host of papers (see Arthur, 1989; or David, 1985) argue that the long-run standard is determined by a series of historical events, which drift the population of users into a specific technology which, by virtue of its stand-alone value, may not have any intrinsic merit. Instead, its only reason for preminence is extrinsic and *ex post*; that is, the fact that many people have already chosen it. Because users want compatibility with the installed base, better products that arrive later may be unable to displace poorer, but earlier standards. Moreover, 'network markets'are 'tippy': the coexistence of incompatible products may be unstable, with a single winning standard dominating the market. This property of 'network markets' can also characterize markets with economies of scale or learning effects. However, in the case of network externalities it is not the level of current sales or cumulative sales that determine the winner. Instead, expectations about the size of a network become crucial.

Another branch of the literature has indeed stressed the role of multiple, self-fulfilling expectations (see Katz and Shapiro, 1986b, 1992; Matsuyama, 1991), in the sense that once individuals believe that a 'critical mass' will lock into a particular standard, it is in their best interest to choose the same standard as well, leading to multiple consistent beliefs and, hence, to multiple equilibria. Therefore, the technological standard is indeterminate and, in particular, not easily related to the underlying characteristics of the set of technological standards that are *ex ante* available. Moreover, since buyers' purchase decisions are strongly influenced by their forecasts of future sales, there can be rewards to affecting these expectations. In these circumstances, the dominant standard need not be the better or cheaper product: an inferior product may be able to defeat a superior one just because it is widely expected to do so.

In this chapter we examine the 'bandwagon' mechanism again and consider a dynamic formulation. We consider a simple framework which allows the description of several kinds of network externalities; that is, it can be viewed as a reduced form of different models with different kinds of network externalities. We assume that there is a continuum of heterogeneous potential adopters and that benefits from adoption depend positively on the proportion of adoptions. Each agent is assumed to have complete information regarding the others' benefit function.

The focus of this chapter is on the equilibrium adoption path of technological standards. A qualitative characterization of the equilibrium adoption path is indeed the main contribution of this chapter: we show that if network externalities are sufficiently strong, then the equilibrium adoption path is discontinuous and a catastrophe point can originate. This result cannot be obtained without increasing returns to adoption.

This chapter is organized as follows. Section 3.2 presents the model and proves the existence of an equilibrium adoption path for two technological standards. Section 3.3 shows under which circumstances the equilibrium adoption path is discontinuous. Section 3.4 contains some further remarks about this literature.

3.2.   THE MODEL

We consider two standards, α and β, which have to be adopted by a continuum of potential adopters. At a particular point in time t each agent has to decide which standard to adopt. Every period the choice is for that period only, and choices are reversible. We assume that such decision is influenced by consideration of the magnitude of the net externalities, which are positively correlated with the proportion of adoptions: there are benefits from compatibility.

Firms are heterogeneous with respect to the effectiveness of the choice of the technological standard on their profits. Let v_α be a parameter measuring the inherent net benefit that a firm would derive from selecting α, and v_β be the analogous parameter for β. Define $v = v_\alpha - v_\beta$. The higher and positive is v, the more preferred α is; the lower and negative is v, the more preferred β is. We assume that each agent is characterized by a parameter v and that v is distributed according to the function $F(v)$, which is smooth, has a finite and convex support (v^1, v^h), where $F(v^1) = 0, F(v^h) = 1$, and is increasing in v.

Let $\Pi_i(v_i, x_i(t), h(t))$ be the net profit flow obtained upon adoption at time t of standard i, where x_i denotes the proportion of adoptions of i, so that $x_\beta = 1 - x_\alpha$, and h is a parameter of profitability, which we assume increases over time $(\partial h / \partial t > 0)$. Let us make the following assumptions:

Assumptions

$$\Pi_\alpha(v_\alpha, x_\alpha, h) = v_\alpha + f(x_\alpha, h) \tag{3.1}$$

$$\Pi_\beta(v_\beta, x_\beta, h) = v_\beta + g(x_\beta, h). \tag{3.2}$$

$f(.)$ and $g(.)$ are smooth and unbounded. Moreover, we have $\partial \Pi_i / \partial x_i > 0, \partial \Pi_i / \partial h > 0$ for $i = \alpha, \beta$, and $\partial f / \partial h > \partial g / \partial h$.

Assumptions (3.1) and (3.2) capture the fact that the net benefits from adopting a standard are both 'inherent' benefits and 'system-use' benefits. That is, the effectiveness of a standard is measured by the parameter v_i and by the benefits deriving from the network externalities. The additive formulation in expressions (3.1) and (3.2) is a simplifying one, and appears in most papers in the literature on network externalities. The signs of the derivatives have a straightforward interpretation: the net profit obtained upon adoption increases the larger the inherent net benefit, and the larger the proportion of adoptions of that standard. The assumption $\partial \Pi_i / \partial h > 0$ implies that there exists learning: over time, knowledge about standard i increases and the benefits upon adoption increase as well. This is a crucial assumption in this model. It is a reasonable assumption if we consider the case of 'unsponsored' innovations, as in Arthur (1989); that is, innovations which do not compete strategically, so that they cannot be priced and manipulated. Indeed, in this case, we can assume that the conditions of supply are sufficiently stable so that the increasing trend in benefits is not reversed. Arbitrarily, we put $\partial f / \partial h > \partial g / \partial h$ which implies that the relative profitability due to learning is larger for α than for β.

Each agent chooses the standard associated with the highest discounted value of expected profits over an infinite horizon. The basic functional equation is:

$$V(x_\alpha, h) = \max_{i \in \{\alpha, \beta\}} W_i(x_i, h)$$

where

$$W_i(x_i, h) = \Pi_i(v_i, x_i, h) + \delta V(x_\alpha^e, h + \mathrm{d}h)$$

where δ denotes the discount factor and x_α^e the expectation over the size of the network for α (and therefore for β, given that $x_\beta = 1 - x_\alpha$).

In what follows we assume that the size of the network expected at a future time is exactly equal to the size of the network which turned out to be optimal at the previous time. Let $P = W_\alpha - W_\beta$, which under our specification of expectations becomes:

$$P(v, x_\alpha, h) = v + f(x_\alpha, h) - g(1 - x_\alpha, h). \tag{3.3}$$

If $P > 0$ at t, then standard α will be chosen, while if $P < 0$ then standard β will be chosen. $P = 0$ is the case of indifference between α and β. Since benefits at time t depend only on the proportion of adoption at time t, we can begin by looking at the static problem of finding the equilibrium values of x_a (and x_β) for each value of t.

For a given h let $v^* = v^*(x_\alpha, h)$ be a threshold value such that $P(v^*, x_\alpha, h) = v^* + f(x_\alpha, h) - g(1 - x_\alpha, h) = 0$. In equilibrium, all types v for whom $P > 0$ will adopt standard α. We have the following:

Definition 1

For a given h a (static) equilibrium is defined by the pair (x_α, x_β) such that:

$$x_\alpha = 1 - F(v^*(x_\alpha, h)) \tag{3.4}$$
$$x_\beta = 1 - x_\alpha \doteq F(v^*(x_\alpha, h)). \tag{3.5}$$

Indeed, for those types with $v > v^*$, we have $P > 0$ and therefore adoption of α is preferred. The proportion of firms whose best response is to adopt standard α at time t is $\int_{v^*}^{v^?} dF(v) = (1 - F(v^*(x_\alpha, h)))$, which in equilibrium must be equal to the proportion of firms who actually adopted at or before time t, as in (3.4). Analogously, for those types with $v < v^*$, adoption of β is preferred. The proportion of these adopters is $\int_{v1}^{v^*} dF(v) = F(v^*(x_\alpha, h))$, which in equilibrium must be equal to the proportion of agents who actually adopted at or before t, as in (3.5). An equilibrium adoption path for the two technological standards is a vector $x(t) = (x_\alpha(t), x_\beta(t))$ for all t. The following proposition holds:

Proposition 3.1

There exists an equilibrium adoption path for the two technological standards.

Proof

Define $Y(x_\alpha, h) = 1 - F(v^*(x_\alpha, h))$. For each h, $Y(x_\alpha, h)$ is continuous in x_α. (Apply the implicit function theorem to $P(v^*, x_\alpha, h) = 0$). Moreover, $Y(x_\alpha, h)$ is defined for all $x_\alpha \in [0, 1]$. Therefore, there exists at least one fixed point, for any h, such that $x_\alpha = Y(x_\alpha, h)$. Then, there exists also at least one fixed point for x_β, such that $x_\beta = F(v^*(x_\alpha, h))$, given that $x_\beta = 1 - x_\alpha$.

Observe that $Y(x_\alpha, h)$ is increasing in x_α and in h. Analogously, $F(v^*(x_\alpha, h)$ is decreasing in x_α and in h (and increasing in x_α).

3.3. THE CHARACTERISTICS OF THE EQUILIBRIUM ADOPTION PATH

In this section we give a characterization of the equilibrium adoption path. Fixed points are shown in Figure 3.1 and Figure 3.2, where we have graphed $Y(x_\alpha, h)$. Now what the equilibrium adoption path looks like depends on the properties of $F_0 v^*$ in h and how one selects among multiple fixed points. Here we want to examine whether the presence of network externalities, and therefore of benefits from compatibility, yields an equilibrium adoption path whose characteristics markedly differ from the case of diffusion with no network externalities.

When there are no network externalities, that is $\partial \Pi_i / \partial x_i = 0$, we get $\partial Y / \partial x_\alpha = 0$, that is, we have just one fixed point; x_α is a single-valued increasing function of h, and therefore there is a unique equilibrium adoption path, which is continuous. For sufficiently high network externalities we get $\partial Y / \partial x_\alpha \gg 0$, which may yield multiple fixed points. For different values of h we can draw the equilibrium adoption path which can look like Figure 3.3.

In Figure 3.3 the graph has two branches and the two points A and B are called fold-points, because these are the points where the combined graph folds over. This is just an informal explanation of what we mean by saying that network externalities can act as a splitting factor, because there is a qualitative change from the case of no network externalities to the situation represented in Figure 3.3.

We can characterize the equilibrium adoption path more rigorously with the tools of catastrophe theory (see Chapter 2, section 2.3). To

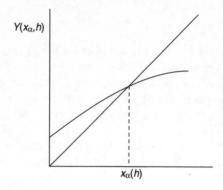

Figure 3.1   The equilibrium adoption path: one fixed point

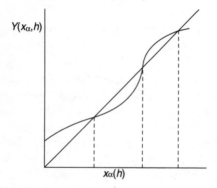

Figure 3.2   The equilibrium adoption path: multiple fixed points

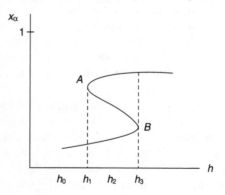

Figure 3.3   The equilibrium adoption path: fold-points

formulate the equilibrium analysis above into the standard framework of catastrophe theory we need to show that the equilibrium defined by (3.4) and (3.5) minimizes a potential function. That is, the dynamic system:

$$dx_\alpha/dt = \varphi_1(x_\alpha, h) = x_\alpha(t) - 1 + F(v^*(x_\alpha(t), h(t))$$
$$dx_\beta/dt = \varphi_2(x_\alpha, h) = 1 - x_\alpha(t) - F(v^*(x_\alpha(t), h(t)) = -\varphi_1(x_\alpha, h)$$

must be a gradient system. This means that there must be some function K, such that $\varphi_1(x_\alpha, h) = -\partial K(x_\alpha, h)/\partial x_\alpha$. Then the equilibria of the system:

$$dx_\alpha/dt = \varphi_1(x_\alpha, h) = -\partial K(x_\alpha, h)/\partial x_\alpha \qquad (3.6)$$
$$dx_\beta/dt = -\varphi_1(x_\alpha, h) = \partial K(x_\alpha, h)/\partial x_\alpha \qquad (3.7)$$

are precisely the singularities of K; that is, x_α, x_β are equilibria iff $\partial K(x_\alpha, h)/\partial x_\alpha = 0$. Thus, the study of how the nature of the system ((3.6) and also (3.7)) changes as t changes can be reduced to the study of the singularities of $K(x_\alpha, h)$. Since $\varphi_1(x_\alpha, h)$ is continuous in x_α it follows that $dx_\alpha/dt = \varphi_1(x_\alpha, h), dx_\beta/dt = -\varphi_1(x_\alpha, h)$ is a gradient system.

Points in the graph of the equilibrium correspondence where the tangent is vertical are the singular points, or catastrophe points. A necessary condition for the equilibrium adoption path to look like Figure 3.3 is that there exists a singular point. This occurs when the following condition is satisfied:

Definition 2

A singular point is characterized by the condition:

$$\frac{\partial F}{\partial v}(v^*(x_\alpha, h)) \frac{\partial P(v^*(x_\alpha, h), x_\alpha, h)/\partial x_\alpha}{\partial P(v^*(x_\alpha, h), x_\alpha, h)/\partial v} = 1. \qquad (3.8)$$

Condition (3.8) easily follows from the fact that $Y(x_\alpha, h)$ must be tangent to x_α in order to have a singular point (see Figure 3.3). We are now in a position to prove the following Proposition:

Proposition 3.2

(i) If $\partial Y/\partial x_\alpha < 1$ at all fixed points, as defined by expression (3.4), then there is a unique equilibrium adoption path, which is continuous.

(ii) The condition $\partial Y/\partial x_\alpha > 1$ at some fixed point, that is, strong network externalities or relative homogeneity among potential adopters, is a sufficient condition for the existence of a catastrophe point. In this case the equilibrium adoption path is discontinuous.

Proof

Part (i)

From the index theorem it follows that if $\partial Y/\partial x_\alpha < 1$ at all fixed points, then there can be only one static equilibrium. By varying h, we get a continuous equilibrium adoption path, which is unique.

Part (ii)

Condition (3.8) certainly occurs if we have $\partial Y/\partial x_\alpha > 1$ at some fixed point, which means that $\partial Y/\partial x_\alpha > 1$ is a sufficient condition for the existence of a catastrophe point. If we compute:

$$\partial Y/\partial x_\alpha = \frac{\partial F}{\partial v} \frac{\partial v^*(x_\alpha, h)}{\partial x_\alpha} = \frac{\partial F}{\partial v} \frac{\partial P(v^*(x_\alpha, h), x_\alpha, h)/\partial x_\alpha}{\partial P(v^*(x_\alpha, h), x_\alpha, h)/\partial v}$$

we get that $\partial Y/\partial x_\alpha > 1$ implies, other things being equal, high density of agents of a given type $(\partial F/\partial v)$ or strong network externalities $(\partial P/\partial x_\alpha)$.

Observe that if $\partial Y/\partial x_\alpha > 1$ at some fixed point, then we have multiple static equilibria. It implies that $x_\alpha(t)$ is a correspondence, not a function. In Figure 3.3 let us envisage a situation in which the values of h are increasing, until the lowest branch terminates at point B, where it has to jump to the other branch. The equilibrium adoption path is therefore discontinuous. Analogously, we get a discontinuity if we let the values of h decrease, until the highest branch terminates at point A, where it has to jump to the lower branch again.

The question arises: what is the economic meaning of possible jumps from one branch to the other of the graphs of the equilibrium correspondence? If one supposes that agents make their own decision at time t, based on the extent of adoption at time $t - \varepsilon$, ε small, that is, each agent expects the proportion of adoptions at time t to be close to what it was at time $t - \varepsilon$, then there exists a unique equilibrium adoption path, given by the lower envelope of the increasing branches of the graph of the equilibrium correspondence. The discontinuity of the equilibrium adoption path can be explained by the fact that if network externalities are sufficiently strong or there is a high density of agents of type α, then the proportion x_α has a sudden jump (a 'bandwagon' effect towards α). As in the 'critical mass' models (see for example, Granovetter and Soong, 1986) there is threshold value over which a large number of adopters coordinate simultaneously on α – a result which recalls what Farrell and Saloner (1985) obtain in a different framework.

3.4.   FURTHER REMARKS

There are further considerations we have to pay attention to when modelling the adoption of technological standards. For example, our assumption of a continuum of potential adopters does not allow us to consider the case where agents behave strategically. However, in systems markets, even more so than in other markets, a firm has strong incentives to build up consumer beliefs about its own system, and to tear down consumer beliefs about rival systems, in trying to tip the market in its own favour. Firms with established reputations, well-known brand names, and visible access to capital have competitive advantages. One would expect firms' strategic behaviour to be used quite aggressively in systems competition. Such behaviour encompasses a wide spectrum: pricing over time, quality choice, degree of compatibility with others, vertical integration into (or from) complementary products, provision of product variety, date of new product introductions, licensing arrangements, and so on. Katz and Shapiro (1985) have examined the incentives for compatibility in a dynamic framework. They show that when firms produce incompatible products, there may be extremely intense competition among producers in the early stages of industry evolution, as each seeks to get ahead of its rivals by building up an installed base. With compatible products, however, all brands are part of a single network; hence there is no mechanism by which a firm may establish a lead in terms of installed base. In other words, compatibility may serve to diminish competition in a system market.

In our model we assume that adopters have complete information with regard to the benefit of adoption; that is to say, there is no uncertainty. Especially, we assume rational expectations about the size of the network. This assumption, quite restrictive, is common to the literature about the dynamics of allocation under increasing returns to adoption occasioned by learning effects or coordination effects.

Katz and Shapiro (1986b) consider a static version of the problem of competing networks of different standards in which network externalities accrue to increased network size. It pays firms to provide large networks if potential adopters expect these networks to be large and thereby commit their choice to them. If, prior to adoption, sufficient numbers of agents believe that network α will have a large share of adopters, it will; but if sufficient numbers believe that network β will have a large share, then it will. They show that multiple 'fulfilled-expectation' equilibria can arise; that is, multiple sets of eventual network adoption shares that fulfil prior expectations. In their model expectations are given and fixed before the adoption process takes place.

More realistically, if firms are affected by future innovation choice decisions, one should assume they would form beliefs about these decisions. Firms might then have conditional probabilities of future states and they might base their choices on these beliefs, which will be updated according to the actual stochastic process.

4 Exit from Lock-in and Market Information

4.1. SELF-REINFORCING MECHANISMS AND 'RECONTRACTING' PROCESSES

Path-dependent dynamic systems with self-reinforcing mechanisms often have a multiplicity of possible asymptotic states. The initial state and early random events push the dynamics into the domain of one of these asymptotic states and thus select the structure that the system eventually locks into. This issue has been tackled in several economic examples, by Arthur, David and others, dealing with sequential choices between competing technologies when increasing returns to adoption are present. These models have shown that such systems display the properties of multiple equilibria, possible inefficiency, lock-in, path-dependence and symmetry-breaking which we introduced in Chapter 1, section 1.2. A question arising in this context is the following: if an economic system is locked-in to an inferior local equilibrium, is 'escape' into a superior one possible? Do we need policies for the economic system, or will spontaneous actions at a local level suffice?

An answer depends on the degree to which the advantages accrued by the inferior equilibrium are transferable to an alternative (see also Arthur, 1988b). If learning effects and specialized fixed costs are the source of the self-reinforcing mechanisms, advantages are not usually transferable to an alternative equilibrium. Indeed, under these dynamic economies of scale there are irreversibilities and exit from lock-in can be very costly. If coordination effects which confer advantages from compatibility with other firms are the source of lock-in, often advantages are transferable. For example, users of a technological standard may agree that an alternative would be better, provided that everybody switched. If the current standard is not embodied in specialized equipment and its advantage is mainly that of commonality of convention, then a changeover to a superior collective choice can provide an escape into the new equilibrium at negligible costs. It has been shown (Farrell and Saloner, 1985) that, in the presence of network externalities, that is when the benefits from adoption of a given technological standard increase with the number of other utilizers purchasing the same standard or compatible items (size of the network), and so long as firms know other firms' preferences, a coordinated changeover can occur (the 'bandwagon' effect). If all users would be better off on the new technology, then they will all switch. If their preferences differ, then the early movers have considerable power to determine the outcome, because of the 'bandwagon' effect itself. However, when preferences are not perfectly known, and each user can choose to switch or not at each period, 'excess inertia' can arise: all prefer the new technology, but none switch. With incomplete information about others' preferences and intentions, no user can be sure that it would be followed in a switch to the new standard. Such uncertainty leads all the users to remain with the status quo even if they all favour switching, because they are unwilling to risk switching without being followed. This is most likely when network externalities are strong and there is a great deal of uncertainty about whether a lead would be followed. Under these circumstances, permanent lock-in to an inferior local equilibrium may occur.

The question about technological switching in the presence of benefits arising from network externalities seems to be particularly relevant, since the issues of compatibility and standardization have become more important than ever. This is especially true within the computer and telecommunications industries, which are characterized by urgent demands for compatibility, and innovations of new products and services, which occur more and more rapidly. The cost that firms incur to achieve compatibility is often small, almost negligible compared with the benefits to be gained from compatibility (Katz and Shapiro, 1985). This is especially true when it is possible to use standardized interfaces, by which we mean that each firm produces according to its own specifications, but that the products of different firms may use the same software or be capable of communicating with one another.

The possibility of 'excess inertia' has been studied also in another paper by Farrell and Saloner (1986b) where timing has an essential role. They suppose that old users do not switch to the new standard, and that the new network must be built up by the adoption decisions of new users, who arrive in the market at a finite rate, imposing delays in achieving a satisfactory network. Of course, the incompatibility costs of these delays are borne by the first users mainly, who may be discouraged to adopt the new standard: the new standard is less likely to succeed the more important the transient incompatibility costs and the larger the installed base. However, their analysis does not exclude the opposite phenomenon, of 'excess momentum': it is early choosers' preferences and expectations that determine the final outcome, so that if these pivotal users find the new standard attractive and adopt it, then they will strand the users who were committed to the old standard. Moreover, if one standard is proprietary, its sponsor may be able to take actions to affect future adoptions of the new standard. Katz and Shapiro (1986a) have studied the case where the installed base is important and there is 'sponsorship' of one or both technologies, so that strategic pricing or cross-subsidization between early and late users can be considered. In their model there is a tendency towards 'excess momentum', in the sense that the technology that will be cheaper later on is likely to prevail over the one which is better in early periods. A striking result that emerges from these analyses is that both 'excess momentum' and 'excess inertia' are equally possible outcomes, which implies that we do not have a definite answer to the problem of technological switching.

In this chapter we consider again the problem of technological switching in the presence of network externalities. We discuss this problem within a class of models allowing 'recontracting' in the market, once it has formed. As we said in Chapter 1, section 1.3, such an approach assumes an already formed market, of fixed size, divided among different categories. Transitions of units between categories are possible, with probabilities that depend on the numbers in each category. Following a common approach in stochastic modelling and taking advantage of certain approximation results in the theory of population processes, we will represent the actions of a firm by a random process in order to draw inferences about the 'macroscopic' behaviour of the system as a whole, which will be almost deterministic. Hence we will let transitions between technologies occur as a Markov process, with transition intensities depending on the market shares of each technology that is on their network. This allows for self-reinforcement. The form of these transition intensities will be derived from the decision process followed by the firms, under certain information constraints.

The purpose of this chapter is twofold. One is to give the technical conditions for there to be multiple equilibria in market share, and for permanent lock-in to one of these equilibria not to occur. The second is to develop a general framework for analyzing the group dynamics, and to introduce to the economic literature some approximation techniques to solve the resulting stochastic model and to characterize the probability distribution of the fraction of agents adopting the same decision.

This chapter is organized as follows. In section 4.2 we construct a stochastic model for the decision rules of the firms and derive a tractable approximation. Our main result is in section 4.3, where we define the stochastic attractiveness of each standard, and show how these determine the number and position of market equilibria. We find that, under certain conditions, permanent lock-in to one of multiple equilibria does not occur when the source of lock-in advantages is network externalities. Instead the system lingers at prevalence of one standard, with intermittent transitions to prevalence of the other. The sojourn time at one of a number of possible system equilibria is calculated in section 4.4 with large deviations methods. Section 4.5 concludes with some examples.

4.2. THE MODEL

We consider the case of two technological standards, denoted by 0 and 1, which are substitutable. There are N firms in the industry which have to decide whether to stay with their present standard or to switch to an alternative, given that there are benefits to be obtained from compatibility. We assume that this is a market-mediated effect; that is, a complementary good becomes cheaper and more readily available the greater the extent of the compatible market. Benefits from compatibility then arise if firms are able to exploit economies of scale in using a common supplier of a complementary good.

Let $n(t) \in 0, \ldots N$ be the number of firms with standard 1, so that the remaining $N - n$ firms must have standard 0. In what follows we will deal with proportions, and so let $y = n/N$ be the proportion of the N firms which have standard 1.

Let us suppose first that all firms have complete information as to the current state of the system and its future dynamics. If the standard employed by a firm is denoted j then, assuming benefits from compatibility, the firm has an action rule $a(j, y) \in \{1 - j, j\}$ (the standard to be employed in the future), given by:

$$a(j,y) = \begin{cases} 0 \text{ if } y < c_j \\ 1 \text{ otherwise} \end{cases} \tag{4.1}$$

where the thresholds c_0 and c_1 differ if there are costs incurred in switching standards. The rule (4.1), in addition to the assumption of perfect information, implies that if all firms are interchangeable, lock-in to a local equilibrium is inevitable. In what follows, we show that supposing that firms have imprecise information about the market position is equivalent to a stochastic formulation, and this allows for 'escape' when multiple equilibria are possible. There are many ways in which to motivate a stochastic model for this problem, and we shall present two in the following subsections.

4.2.1. A Game-Theoretic Approach

We shall allow movement between the alternatives to occur as a *stochastic strategy revision process* (see, for example, Blume, 1993), where all firms are considered to be neighbours. Strategy revision opportunities occur for each firm as independent Poisson processes with rate v. This can be rationalized as being due, for example, to the expiration of contracts, availability of funds, frequency of market surveys or change of management.

At each revision opportunity a firm determines its simple best response strategy by playing a symmetric 2 x 2 game with every other firm. The payoff matrix can be written as:

$$G = \begin{bmatrix} a & b \\ c & d \end{bmatrix}$$

where, to ensure benefits from compatibility, we have $\min\{a,d\} > \max\{b,c\}$. If we denote by p_{ij} the probability that at a revision opportunity a firm currently with choice i chooses choice j, then we obtain a stochastic choice model by setting the log-odds of choosing each strategy equal to a function of the difference in average payoffs, that is,

$$\log\frac{p_{01}(y)}{p_{00}(y)} = f(\alpha g(y) - \gamma_1), \quad \log = \frac{p_{10}(y)}{p_{11}(y)} = f(-\alpha g(y) - \gamma_0),$$

$$\tag{4.2}$$

(neglecting terms of $O(1/N)$), where $g(y) = -a + c + (a - b - c + d)y$, γ_i is the cost to switch to standard i, and α is a parameter corresponding to the forecast horizon. If we now define $\lambda(y)$ and $\mu(y)$ by:

$$\lambda(y) = vp_{01}(y), \qquad \mu(y) = p_{10}(y) \tag{4.3}$$

then $\lambda(y)$ and $\mu(y)$ can be calculated from (4.2). The above construction is of course equivalent to supposing that the transitions $0 \rightarrow 1$ and $1 \rightarrow 0$ occur for each firm as independent Poisson process with rates $\lambda(y)$ and $\mu(y)$ respectively. There remains the problem of selecting a function $f(.)$ in (4.2). For example, the following function:

$$f(x) = \log \frac{e^x}{v - e^x} \tag{4.4}$$

is consistent with the notion of network externalities, yielding:

$$\lambda = v \exp(\alpha g(y) - \gamma_1), \qquad \mu = v \exp(-\alpha g(y) - \gamma_0) \tag{4.5}$$

which are suitably convex. As we shall see in section 4.3, this choice provides for sufficiently diverse system behaviour and, indeed, a more complex dependence of the transition intensities on y might result in behaviour with no rational interpretation. Note that (4.4) introduces the requirement that

$$v \geq \{\exp(\alpha(d - b) - \gamma_1), \exp(\alpha(a - c) - \gamma_0)\}.$$

4.2.2. A Stochastic Control Theory Approach

Let us suppose now that strategy revision opportunities occur independently for each firm as Poisson process of rate v, and at such an opportunity at time t, if the firm currently operates standard j, then they must choose an action $a \in \{1 - j, j\}$, either changing their standard or retaining the present standard. The cost function for the period until the next revision opportunity is then:

$$C(y, a, T) = \delta(a, 1 - j)\gamma_{1-j} - \int_t^{t+T} R_j(y) dy(\tau) \tag{4.6}$$

where $T \sim \exp(\nu)$ and $R_j(y)$ is the anticipated rate of returns from operating standard j with system state y. Now let us suppose that between revision opportunities the state of the system changes in accordance with the kernel:

$$P_a^T(y, \mathrm{d}y) = \mathrm{prob}(y(t + T) \in \mathrm{d}y | y(t) = y, a(t) = a). \tag{4.7}$$

Firms will now attempt to formulate a policy π to minimize the expected discounted cost

$$V_\pi(y) = E_\pi(\Sigma_{i=0}^{\infty}(\int_{T_i}^{T_{i+1}} \alpha^{T_i + \tau} \mathrm{d}\tau)C(y(T_i), a(T_i)T_{i+1} - T_i) | y(0) = y) \tag{4.8}$$

where $\alpha \in (0, 1)$ is the discount factor. The optimal cost function $V_\alpha(y)$ will thus obey the recursion:

$$V_\alpha(y) = \min_a \{C(y, a, T) + \alpha \int_0^1 P_a^T(y, d\zeta) V_\alpha(\zeta)\}. \tag{4.9}$$

Then the optimal policy will be of the form:

$$a = \begin{cases} 0 \text{ if } y < c_j(R, P, \alpha) \\ 1 \text{ otherwise} \end{cases}$$

where the thresholds c_j are functions of anticipated rate of return $R(.)$ and the transition kernel P, and where $c_0(.) \geq c_1(.)$, with strict inequality provided that $\min\{\gamma_0, \gamma_1\} > 0$. Although $c_j(.)$ is a deterministic function of P and R, these latter quantities differ between firms, and thus, as the revision opportunities occur in a Poisson process with the same rate for all firms, considered from the viewpoint of the system as a whole, P and R (and hence $c_j(.)$) may be taken to be random variables at any given revision opportunity. In other words, we can model the system by allowing revision opportunities to occur as above, and then switching standards with probabilities $p_{ij}(y)$, derived from knowledge of $R(.)$ and $P(.)$. If we again define $\lambda(y)$ and $\mu(y)$ by (4.3), then we have the same stochastic process as obtained in subsection 4.2.1, but possibly with greater generality regarding the forms of $\lambda(.)$ and $\mu(.)$.

This approach is also useful in rationalizing observed system behaviour where one standard greatly predominates, in which case firms might be observed to change standard, and then change back. Although a single firm might make two consecutive transitions, there will almost certainly have been many decisions made in the interim, so firms are not continuously changing standard. Moreover, the interchangeability of the firms means that the same firm will almost certainly not be the next to change from the predominant standard. Finally, such 'experimentation' is an inevitable consequence of a stochastic formulation. It can be variously rationalized as a willingness to experiment, or the possibility of 'error' in the estimate of future trends and/or returns.

4.2.3. The Long-time Behaviour of the Market

We are now in a position to summarize the structure of the model. For a single firm we can represent the decision process (or more accurately the actions resulting from it) by a stochastic process, specifically a two-state (indexed by standard) Markov chain in continuous time, with transition intensities $\lambda(y)$ and $\mu(y)$ for the transitions $0 \rightarrow 1$ and $1 \rightarrow 0$ respectively. This stochastic formulation is equivalent to operating the decision rule (4.1) on the basis of imprecise knowledge of y, and this can be explained as follows.

Suppose that a firm is in state '0', then formally, in a small time interval Δt (identical for all firms), in which a firm makes exactly one decision, we have:

$$\text{prob}(0) = 1 - \lambda(y)\Delta t + 0(\Delta t), \ \text{prob}(1) = \lambda(y)\Delta t + 0(\Delta t). \quad (4.10)$$

If we define a correct action by the rule (4.1) the stochastic firm can make two types of error, namely move to the other standard when the correct action is stay with the current standard, and vice versa. Let us denote the probability of an error by ε_0, then from (4.10) we obtain:

$$\varepsilon_0(y) = \begin{cases} \lambda(y)\Delta t, & y \leq c_0 \\ 1 - \lambda(y)\Delta t, & y > c_0 \end{cases}$$

which is equivalent to operating the decision rule (4.1) with the 'perfect information' y replaced by 'imperfect information' in the form of a random variable X with distribution given by:

$$\text{prob}(X \le x) = \begin{cases} \varepsilon(c_0 - y + x) & 0 \le x \le y \\ 1 - \varepsilon_0(c_0 - y + x), & y < x < 1 \\ 1 & x = 1 \end{cases}$$

A similar random variable Z can be defined for a firm in state '1', with analogous dependence on $\mu(y)$.

Some properties of the transition intensities are listed here.

$\lambda(.)$ and $\mu(.)$ are bounded and Lipschitz continuous.   (A1)

$\partial\mu(z)/\partial z < 0 < \partial(z)/\partial z$ (A2)

Assumption (A1) is required for technical reasons. In actual fact, $\lambda(.)$ and $\mu(.)$ are only defined on the points $S = \{0, 1/N, \dots (N-1)/N, 1\}$ so, without loss of generality, we will take $\lambda(z)$ and $\mu(z)$ to be Lipschitz continuous functions through the points $\{\lambda(S)\}$ and $\{\mu(S)\}$. Assumption (A2) captures the fact that agents benefit from increasing compatibility.

Obviously, $n(t)$ is a birth–death process, hence is reversible, with an easily obtained (static) equilibrium distribution (see Kelly, 1979). However, this result is not amenable to interpretation, and worse, tells us nothing about the dynamics of the process, which are the object of interest. Further, the birth–death process solution is impossible to implement in the case of more than two standards, while the method we will propose can be extended, although some numerical computation may be required.

The process $y(t)$ is a Markov process with generator (see Whittle, 1986):

$$L_N f(z) = N(1-z)\lambda(z)[f(z + 1/N) - f(z)] \\ + Nz\mu(z)[f(z - 1/N) - f(z)] \tag{4.11}$$

which is very nearly first-order for large N. Formally, Taylor's expansion yields:

$$L_N f = a(z)\partial f/\partial z + (1/2N)b(z)\partial^2 f/\partial z^2 + O(1/N^2), \tag{4.12}$$

where $a(z) = (1 - z)\lambda(z) - z\mu(z)$ and $b(z) = (1 - z)\lambda(z) + z\mu(z)$. Now observe that the operator $a(z)\partial/\partial z$ is also the generator of a Markov process, specifically the (unique) deterministic process $z(t)$ which solves the ordinary differential equation:

$$\mathrm{d}z/\mathrm{d}t = (1 - z)\lambda(z) - z\mu(z), \qquad z(0) = y(0). \tag{4.13}$$

The following theorem states that the deterministic process $z(t)$ which solves (4.13) is asymptotically close to the stochastic process $y(t)$.

Theorem (Kurtz (1978))

If the transition intensities $\lambda(z), \mu(z)$ are bounded and Lipschitz continuous then, for any $t > 0, \varepsilon > 0$, there exist positive numbers C_1, C_2 such that

$$\mathrm{prob}(\sup_{0 \le s \le t} |y(s) - z(s)| > \varepsilon) < C_1 e^{-NC_2}$$

Corollary

For all $t \ge 0$ we have $\lim_{N \to \infty} E[y(t)] = z(t)$.

Notwithstanding the theorem stated above, there exists the possibility of $y(t)$ making excursions far from $z(t)$. This is particularly interesting if $z(t)$ has multiple stable fixed points, since the system may be able to 'tunnel' between them. In the main, convergence of the $z(t)$ will imply similar convergence of $y(t)$, and hence our problem can be simplified and reduced to solving the ordinary differential equation (4.13).

Here we are interested in the properties of the stationary solution (where $\mathrm{d}z/\mathrm{d}t = 0$) and in particular how it changes as a result of benefits from compatibility.

The fixed points of (4.13) are the solution(s) z of the equation:

$$\bar{z} = \frac{\lambda(\bar{z})}{\lambda(\bar{z}) + \mu(\bar{z})}. \tag{4.14}$$

If we denote the right-hand side of (4.14) by $F(\bar{z})$, then (A1) and (A2) imply that $F(.)$ is a continuous monotonically increasing function.

Thus solutions of (4.14) occur due to $F(\bar{z})$ alternately crossing the diagonal from above and below, and the non-negativity of the transition intensities and (A2) yield that (4.13) has an odd number of solutions. These observations yield the following result concerning the stability character of the fixed points of $z(t)$:

Proposition 4.1

Let the solutions of the fixed-point equation (4.14) be $0 \leq \bar{z}_0 < \bar{z}_1 < \ldots < \bar{z}_{2m} \leq 1$. Then the points $\bar{z}_{2j}, j = 0, \ldots, m$ are asymptotically stable in the regions $D_0 = [(0, \bar{z}_1), \ldots, D_j = (\bar{z}_{2j=1}, \bar{z}_{2j+1}), \ldots, D_m = (\bar{z}_{2m=1}, 1)]$. The points $\bar{z}_{2j=1}, j = 1, \ldots, m$ are unstable.

Proof

First note that in a one-dimensional system the only possible fixed points are asymptotically stable or unstable. If we take a fixed point $\bar{z}$ of (4.13) and perturb it we obtain the linear perturbation equation:

$$d\zeta/dt = [(1 - \bar{z})\partial\lambda(\bar{z})/\partial z - \lambda(\bar{z}) - \bar{z}\partial\mu(\bar{z})/\partial z - \mu(\bar{z})]\zeta.$$

Appealing to (4.14) we can rewrite this as:

$$d\zeta/dt = -(1 - \partial F(\bar{z})/\partial z)(\lambda(\bar{z}) + \mu(\bar{z}))\zeta.$$

Hence $\bar{z}$ is stable (unstable) if $\partial F(\bar{z})/\partial z < 1 (> 1)$. Observing that $F(.)$ crossing from above (below) implies $\partial F(\bar{z})/\partial z < 1 (> 1)$ completes the proof, the last assertion being obvious from (4.14).

We shall conclude this section by examining the shape of the equilibrium probability distribution. Consider (4.12), taking L_N to $O(N^{-1})$ terms, thus obtaining a diffusion approximation. Then the probability density $\pi(z, t)$ of $z(t)$ obeys the Kolmogorov forward equation (see Whittle, 1986):

$$\partial\pi/\partial t = -\partial(a\pi)/\partial z + (1/2N)/\partial^2(b\pi)/\partial z^2,$$

an equation of the Fokker–Plank type, which has the stationary solution

$$\pi(z) \sim b(z)^{-1} \exp[2N \int_0^z (a(\zeta)/b(\zeta))d\zeta].$$

Since $a(z) = (\lambda(z) + \mu(z))(F(z) - z)$, it is easy to see that the integral is maximized at the stable solution of the fixed-point equation (4.14) and minimized at the unstable solution. Hence $\pi(z)$ is peaked (with increased sharpness as N becomes large) around the stable fixed points of (4.13).

4.3. PSEUDO NETWORK EXTERNALITIES

We will now quantify the effect of compatibility. Recall that the game-theoretic model produced transition intensities of the form

$$\lambda(z) = \lambda(0) \exp(k_1 z), \qquad \mu(z) = \mu(0) \exp(-k_0 z), \tag{4.15}$$

for some constants $k_0 > 0, k_1 > 0$. In the remainder of the section we shall assume (4.15), and will demonstrate that it is sufficient for the purpose of our model. This functional form also occurs in Weidlich and Braun (1991), where the transition intensities are defined in terms of utilities. We observe that (4.15) implicitly imposes the condition:

$$\lambda(0) > 0, \qquad \mu(1) > 0, \tag{4.16}$$

that is, there is a positive probability of switching from a universally operated standard. However, should we wish to consider, for example, the case of $\lambda(0) = 0$, we shall take $\lambda(z) \cong k_1^{-1} \exp(k_1 z)$, and consider the large k_1 limit. Similarly, should we wish $\mu(1) = 0$, we need only consider the large k_0 limit of $\mu(z) \cong k_0^{-1} \exp(k_0(1 - z))$. Alternatively, since (4.16) is obviously just the requirement that neither standard can be eliminated from the system, we could rationalize it by expanding the model to include inactive firms (that do not change), with vested interests in each of the standards. The state y then becomes merely the proportion of active firms with standard 1.

Supposing the form (4.15), the following definition provides a measure, via the transition intensities, of the 'stochastic attractiveness' of each standard.

Definition

The pseudo network externalities (PNE) of standard j is σ_j where:

$$\sigma = \log[\mu(0)/\lambda(0)] \qquad \sigma_1 = \log[\lambda(1)/\mu(1)]$$

Taking σ_0, for example, $\mu(0)$ is the maximum intensity for a transition to option 0, while $\lambda(0)$ is the minimum intensity for a transition to option 1; that is, the probability intensity of making a mistake for a firm with standard 0. Thus, σ_j is the difference of the logarithms of a term measuring the network externality and an error term.

The assumption (4.15) implies the identity $\sigma_1 = k_0 + k_1 - \sigma_0$, which together with (4.14) enables us to write:

$$F(z) = \frac{1}{1 + \exp[\sigma_0 - z(\sigma_0 + \sigma_1)]}. \tag{4.17}$$

This has the following immediate consequence:

Proposition 4.2

$F(z)$ is convex (concave) for $z < \omega(z > \omega)$, where $\omega = \sigma_0/(\sigma_0 + \sigma_1)$, and hence the system has at most two stable equilibria.

Proof

The first assertion follows immediately from (4.17), thus (4.14) has at most three solutions by a simple convexity argument and Proposition 4.1 does the rest.

Corollary

If $\sigma_0 + \sigma_1 < 4$ then there is exactly one stable equilibrium.

Proof

First note that if $\omega < 0$, or $\omega > 1$, then (4.14) has only one solution. Otherwise, by (4.17) and the definition of ω, we get:

$\max_z(\partial F(z)/\partial z) = \partial F(\omega)/\partial z = [(\sigma_0 + \sigma_1)\lambda(\omega)\mu(\omega)/(\lambda(\omega) + \mu(\omega))^2] = (\sigma_0 + \sigma_1)/4$. Hence if $\sigma_0 + \sigma_1 < 4$, $\partial F(z)/\partial z < 1$ for all z and (4.14) can only have one solution. Finally, by Proposition 4.1, a solitary fixed point is stable.

The next result is a complement to the corollary to Proposition 4.2. These two results together with Proposition 4.4 show that PNEs completely determine the number of stable equilibria.

Proposition 4.3

If $\sigma_0 = \sigma_1$ then:

(a) $\bar{z} = 1/2$ is a solution of the fixed point equation (4.14).
(b) If $\sigma_o + \sigma_1 > 4$ the system has two stable equilibria.

Proof

Part (a) is immediate from (4.17). By the definition of ω, we get $\omega = 1/2$, and so (see the preceding proof), $\partial F(1/2)/\partial z = (\sigma_0 + \sigma_1)/4$. An appeal to Propositions 4.1 and 4.2 completes the proof of part (b).

The interpretation of Proposition 4.3 and the corollary to Proposition 4.2 is straightforward. If the two standards are equally attractive then $z = 1/2$ (equal market shares) is the unique stable equilibrium provided that the network externalities are sufficiently weak relative to the differences in information available to the firms. If the network externalities are strong (even possibly σ_0 and σ_1 both infinite) then there are two stable equilibria, corresponding to prevalence of each of the standards (a 100 per cent market share if σ_0 and σ_1 are infinite). If the two standards are not equally attractive we have the following similar, but necessarily more complex, result:

Proposition 4.4.

If $\sigma_0 \neq \sigma_1$ then:
(a) If $\sigma_0 > \sigma_1 (\sigma_0 < \sigma_1)$, the system has a stable equilibrium at $\bar{z} < 1/2 (\bar{z} > 1/2)$.

(b) Let $B_0 = \min_{0 < \beta < \sigma_1} [(\beta + \sigma_0)(1 + e^{-\beta})]$, $B_1 = \max_{0 < \beta < 1} [\beta \sigma_0 (1 + e^{(1-\beta)\sigma_0})]$.
Then the fixed-point equation (4.14) has the following properties:
  (i)   if $\sigma_0 < 0$ or $\sigma_1 < 0$ there is exactly one stable equilibrium.
  (ii) if min $\{\sigma_0, \sigma_1\} > 0$ and min $\{\sigma_0, B_0 - \sigma_0\} < \sigma_1 < \max\{\sigma_0,$
        $B_1 - \sigma_0\}$ then there are two stable equilibria.
  (iii) if $0 < \sigma_1 < \min\{\sigma_0, B_0 - \sigma_0\}$ or $0 < \max\{\sigma_0, B_1 - \sigma_0\} < \sigma_1$
        then there is exactly one stable equilibrium.

Proof

Parts (a) and (b)(i) are immediate from Proposition 4.2. Next we suppose that $0 < \sigma_1 < \sigma_0$. Then recalling (4.17) and the definition of ω, since $F(\omega) = 1/2$, (4.14) has a solution $\bar{z}_o < \omega$. To consider the range $\omega < z < 1$, let $z = 1 - (1 - \beta/\sigma_1)(1 - \omega), 0 < \beta < \sigma_1$. Then it is easy to show that $F(z) - z > 0$ for some β (and hence (4.14) has solutions $\bar{z}_1, \bar{z}_2 \in (\omega, 1)$ if and only if $\sigma_0 + \sigma_1 > (\beta + \sigma_0)(1 + e^{-\beta})$, which yields the lower bound involving B_0. Now suppose $\sigma_0 < \sigma_1$. Since $F(\omega) = 1/2$, (4.14) has a solution $\bar{z}_2 > \omega$. Again it is easy to show that $F(\beta\omega) - \beta\omega < 0$ for some $\beta \in (0, 1)$, and hence (4.14) has two solutions $\bar{z}_0, \bar{z}_1 \in (0, \omega)$, if and only if $\sigma_0 + \sigma_1 < o(1 + e^{(1-\beta)\sigma_0})$. This yields the upper bound involving B_1, and parts (ii) and (iii) are then consequences of Proposition 4.1 and Proposition 4.2.

Part (a) simply tells us that there is a stable equilibrium corresponding to prevalence of the more attractive standard. In part (b)(i) the benefits of network externalities for the given standard are small compared with the probability of mistakenly switching, and then the other standard will prevail. Parts (ii) and (iii) show that there will be two stable equilibria provided that the stochastic attractiveness of the two standards do not differ too greatly.

Finally, we have an additional result, the interpretation of which is fairly clear:

Proposition 4.5

(a) If there exist two stable equilibria $\bar{z}_0 < \bar{z}_2$ say, then $\bar{z}_0 < 1/2 < \bar{z}_2$.
(b) If there exists only one stable equilibrium $\bar{z}_0 < 1/2 (> 1/2)$, then $\sigma_0 > \sigma_1 (\sigma_0 < \sigma_1)$.

Proof

The first assertion follows from Proposition 4.3 and from the fact that if $\sigma_0 < \sigma_1$ and $\bar{z}_0 < 1/2$ solves the fixed-point equation (4.14), then (4.14) has another solution $\bar{z}_2$ such that $\bar{z}_2 > 1 - \bar{z}_0$. (This is true because by hypothesis $\bar{z}_0 = F(\bar{z}_0)$, so the assertion is certainly proved if $1 - \bar{z}_0 < F(1 - \bar{z}_0)$. From (4.17) this is true iff $\exp(\sigma_0 - \sigma_1) < 1$). The second assertion is a simple corollary of Proposition 4.2.

Thus, if there is more than one stable equilibrium, then each corresponds to prevalence of a different standard, while if there is only one, the prevalent standard is that with the greater PNE.

4.4. LARGE DEVIATIONS

In cases where more than one stable equilibrium exists it is possible to obtain large deviation-type estimates for the expected time taken for the system to make a transition between them. Following Weiss (1986) the expected time taken to go from a stable equilibrium $\bar{z}$ to an unlikely point v is proportional to $\exp(NI + o(N))$ where I solves the variational problem

$$I = \inf_S \int_{t_1}^{t_2} h(z(t), dz(t)/dt)dt$$

where $h(z, \beta) = \sup_\alpha \{\alpha\beta - (1 - z)\lambda(z)(e^\alpha - 1) - z\mu(z)(e^{-\alpha} - 1)\}$ and $S = \{t_1, t_2, z(t) : z(t_1) = \bar{z}, z(t_2) = v\}$ is the set of all paths from $\bar{z}$ to v. For our model the solution takes the form $I = \int_{\bar{z}}^v \log[z\mu(z)/(1 - z)\lambda(z)]dz$ which can be explicitly calculated as follows:

$$I = (v - \bar{z})\sigma_0 - (v^2 - z^{-2})(\sigma_0 + \sigma_1)/2 + \log[v^v(1 - v)^{(1-v)}]$$
$$- \log[\bar{z}^{\bar{z}}(1 - \bar{z})^{(1-\bar{z})}].$$

From Proposition 4.1 we know that any two stable equilibria are separated by an unstable equilibrium, which we can take as an unlikely point. If $\bar{z}_0, \bar{z}_1, \bar{z}_2$ are stable, unstable, stable respectively, then we can express the system dynamics in the form of the transition intensities:

$$q_N(\bar{z}_0, \bar{z}_2) \cong \exp\{-N \int_{\bar{z}_0}^{\bar{z}_1} \log[z\mu(z)/(1-z)\lambda(z)]dz\}$$

and

$$q_N(\bar{z}_2, \bar{z}_0) \cong \exp\{-N \int_{\bar{z}_2}^{\bar{z}_1} \log[z\mu(z)/(1-z)\lambda(z)]dz$$

Treating this as two-state Markov process the relative likelihoods of the two system equilibria are given by

$$\pi_N(\bar{z}_2)/\pi_N(\bar{z}_0) \cong \exp\{N \int_{\bar{z}_0}^{\bar{z}_2} \log[(1-z)\lambda(z)/z\mu(z)]dz\}. \tag{4.19}$$

With obvious modifications, the same procedure is applicable to any number of stable equilibria. We can now examine the effects of PNEs for large N. The following proposition gives the result for $\sigma_0 < \sigma_1$, but also the obvious complement holds.

Proposition 4.6

Suppose the system has two stable equilibria $\bar{z}_o < 1/2 < \bar{z}_2$. If

$$\sigma_0 < \sigma_1 \text{ then } \lim_{N\to\infty} \frac{\pi_N(\bar{z}_2)}{\pi_N(\bar{z}_0)} = \infty.$$

Proof

Consider expression (4.19). The proposition follows from positivity of

$$\tilde{I} = \int_{\bar{z}_0}^{\bar{z}_2} \log[(1-z)\lambda(z)/z\mu(z)]dz = \int_{\bar{z}_0}^{\bar{z}_2} (\sigma_0 + \sigma_1)z - \sigma_0 + \log[(1-z)/z]dz$$

Since $1 - \bar{z}_0 < \bar{z}_2$ (see the proof of Proposition 4.5), and the integrand is positive over the interval $(1 - \bar{z}_0, \bar{z}_2)$, we get

$$\tilde{I} > \int_{\bar{z}_0}^{1-\bar{z}_0} (\sigma_0 + \sigma_1)z - \sigma_0 + \log[(1-z)/z]dz = \frac{\sigma_1 - \sigma_0}{2}(1 - 2\bar{z}_0) > 0.$$

Thus the predominant equilibria in a large system is that which corresponds to a larger market share of the standard with the greatest PNE.

4.5. EXAMPLES

Before concluding, let us present a few simple examples. Let us take the transition rates (4.5), with $a = 2, b = c = 1, d = 4$, and $\gamma_1 = 2\gamma_2 = \gamma$. Thus, we have

$$\lambda(z) = v\exp(\alpha(4z - 1) - 2\gamma), \qquad \mu(z) = v\exp(\alpha(1 - 4z) - \gamma),$$

which yields $\sigma_0 = 2\alpha + \gamma$ and $\sigma_1 = 6\alpha - \gamma$. Let us consider the following:

Example 1

Take $\alpha = 0.25, \gamma = 0.5$, so that $\sigma_0 = \sigma_1 = 1$. Then the corollary to Proposition 4.2 predicts one stable equilibrium. Figure 4.1 shows the diagram of $F(z)$ against z and Figure 4.2 the unimodal probability density for example 1.

Example 2

Take $\alpha = 0.75, \gamma = 1.5$, so that $\sigma_0 = \sigma_1 = 3$. Then Proposition 4.3 predicts two stable equilibria and Proposition 4.5 tells us that one of these equilibria will have standard 0 in the majority and the other standard 1 predominating. Figure 4.3 shows the diagram of $F(z)$ against z and Figure 4.4 the bimodal probability density for Example 2. One can compute the expected time to go from the lower stable

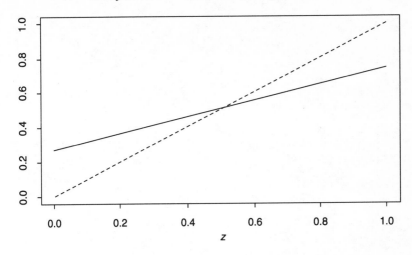

Figure 4.1   Plot of $F(z)$ against z (fixed points of $z(t)$) for Example 1; unique stable fixed point

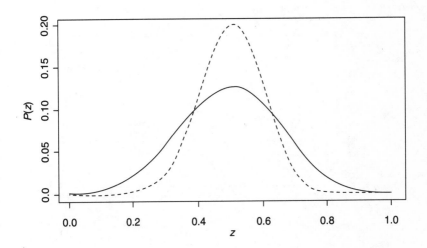

Figure 4.2   Empirical probability density for Example 1; simulation with $N = 20$ (solid line) and $N = 50$ (broken line)

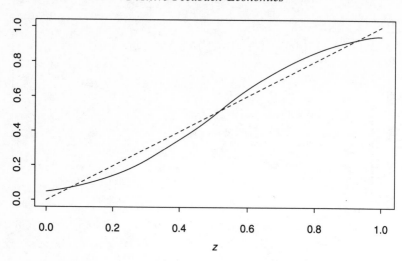

Figure 4.3   Plot of $F(z)$ against z (fixed points of $z(t)$) for Example 2; two
            stable (and one unstable) fixed points

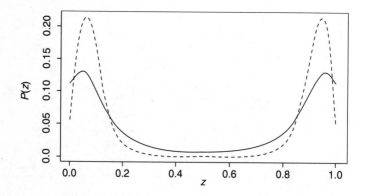

Figure 4.4   Empirical probability density for Example 2; simulation with $N =$
            20 (solid line) and $N = 50$ (broken line)

equilibrium $\bar{z}_0$ to the higher stable equilibrium $\bar{z}_2$ using the technique of section 4.4. From (4.18) we get that the expected time is $T \cong \exp(0.115N + o(N))$. It is impossible to simulate large deviation events for a sufficiently large N to be able to ignore the $o(N)$ term. Figure 4.5 shows logarithms of the simulated times, a least-squares regression fit, and the predictions of expected times as from (4.19), from which it appears that the $o(N)$ term is roughly a constant independent of N in this case.

Example 3

Take $\alpha = \gamma = 1$, so that $\sigma_0 = 3$ and $\sigma_1 = 5$. Proposition 4.4 predicts two stable equilibria and Proposition 4.5 tells us that one of these equilibria will have standard 0 in the majority and the other standard 1 predominating. To compute the expected time the system will take to move from equilibrium $\bar{z}_0$ to the superior equilibrium $\bar{z}_2$ we can again calculate $I = 0.0047$ from (4.18). We get $T \cong \exp(0.0047N + o(N))$. Hence, if revision opportunities arise, on average, once per month, we would expect that a system of 100 firms will take 1.6 months to change from the industry standard of 0 to 1. On the other hand, the reverse movement has $I = 0.9466$, and hence an expected time of 10^{40} years, which is at least an efficient behaviour for the system, given that standard 1 is more attractive.

4.6. FURTHER REMARKS

In this chapter we have studied the problem of switching between two technological standards in the presence of network externalities and imprecise information about the other agents' choices. The main result concerns the situation where there exists a positive probability of switching from a uniformly operated standard. In such a case, if the effect of network externalities is sufficiently strong, the switching costs sufficiently small, and both effects relatively balanced over the two standards, then permanent lock-in to one market position is not possible. Instead, the system makes intermittent transitions, after a sojourn time whose mean can be shown to increase exponentially with the number of firms, between prevalence of each option.

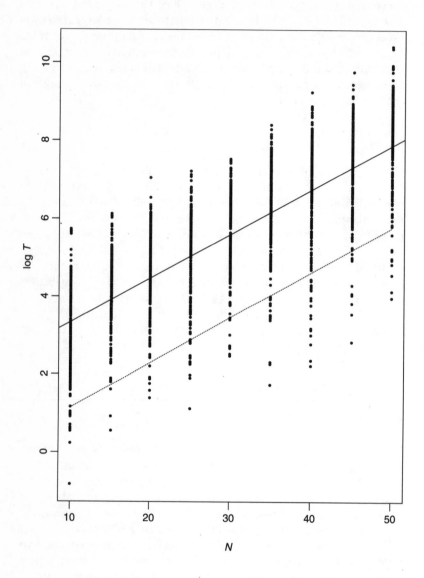

Figure 4.5   Simulated first $\bar{z}_0 \to \bar{z}_2$ passage times for Example 2; least-squares
            fit (solid line) and theoretical predictions (broken line)

For the situation of a possible replacement of one standard by a superior alternative, section 4.3 gives necessary conditions for the new standard to displace the old, and section 4.4 the time such displacement is likely to take. This displacement will be exponentially quick if the new standard is so superior that the only possible stable equilibrium for the system is such that the new standard predominates.

The main contribution of this model is to identify the role of self-reinforcing mechanisms, in the form of network externalities, to get the 'macroscopic' results of a complicated 'microscopic' decision process. The idea is to introduce 'noise' into what would otherwise be a model in which 'excess inertia' is possible. The result is that, with some technical conditions, 'excess inertia' is indeed a transient problem.

Another mechanism to overcome 'excess inertia', which is not considered here, is communication. It seems plausible that allowing even a minimal amount of coordination between the firms would eliminate such inertia. Farrell and Saloner (1985) show that allowing a single public statement by each firm as to whether it favours the switch before any actions are taken eliminates 'excess inertia' provided that the preferences of the firms coincide; otherwise, if preferences differ, inertia increases.

In our model choices are made one at a time, while a more realistic situation is that groups of firms choose at the same time, or coalitions of firms do. As far as we know, there are no models in this literature where the implications of the choice of coalitions of agents is considered. A few insights are in Föllmer (1974) and in Kirman (1983), where the problem of communication and coalitions is studied in a different context, by considering a set of agents and imposing on it a probabilistic structure, according to the graph theories. These papers, however, have not been developed within the context of dynamic stochastic processes, and most of their results are within a static framework.

Finally, observe that when network externalities are embodied in an installed base, an early start or a protected market could in principle lead to a lasting competitive advantage. In this case, substantial changeover costs of switching from one standard to another are likely to be incurred, and can prevent exit from a lock-in position. Such changeover costs can be incorporated in the transition intensities of our model, and can easily lead to the alternative standard being unviable, or to very long expected time for switching.

5 Positive Feedbacks and Lock-in by Random Events

5.1. COMPETING TECHNOLOGIES AND LOCK-IN

It has long been argued that as a result of externalities the value of choosing a technology may be enhanced by the fact that other firms have previously chosen it. This issue has been tackled by Brian Arthur and Paul David in their writings on cumulative causation occurring in path-dependent processes which have affected much of the literature about the dynamics of allocation under increasing returns occasioned by learning-by-doing and learning-by-using phenomena. The idea is that 'history matters' when increasing returns to adoption are intro-duced. If one technology gets ahead by good fortune it gains an advantage, with the result that the adoption market may 'tip' in its favour and may end up dominated by it. With different circumstances, a different technology might have been favoured early on and it might have come to dominate the market. Thus in competition between technologies with increasing returns there are possible multiple equili-bria. As to which actual outcome is selected from these multiple candidate outcomes, it is argued that the prevailing outcome turns out to depend on the path which has been initially chosen. In particular, the resulting outcome may be inefficient; that is, the market may be locked-in to the 'wrong' technology.

There are examples of such situations. In an excellent historical study David (1985) discussed the adoption of the QWERTY keyboard for typewriters. This example is by now a rather famous and intriguing one for economists. In 1873 Cristopher Sholes found that the usual alphabetic arrangement of keys caused his up-strike keyboard mechan-ism to jam and therefore, after considerable experimentation, a differ-ent arrangement was selected that caused typing bars to come up from different directions on most consecutive letters. The first six letters of this new arrangement were QWERTY. In due course, these typewriters were mass-produced, typists learned QWERTY, typing schools taught

QWERTY, employers bought QWERTY, so that manufacturers which failed to adopt such arrangement disappeared from the market very soon. Apparently, the Dvorak keyboard, invented in 1932, is much faster, and yet it has not replaced the less efficient QWERTY keyboard, which still remains the dominant keyboard arrangement.

There are also other examples like this, which come as no surprise to readers of economic history cases. For example, a series of circumstances discussed by Cowan (1990, 1991) acted to favour the construction of light-water nuclear reactors in the USA in the 1950s, so that learning and construction experience gained with light-water early on locked the market in by the mid-1960s; however, the engineering literature argues that, given equal development, the gas-cooled design would have been superior. Similarly, a series of circumstances (Arthur, 1984) gave gasoline enough of a lead as the power source for automobiles, and whether steam and electric cars, given equal development, could have been superior is still not clear. Another example is provided by the video technology Sony Betamax competing over its rival VHS, where industry specialists claim that the loser in the video contest, Betamax, is technically superior to VHS (Arthur, 1988a).

As a simple and basic model of competition between technologies with increasing returns let us consider the model by Arthur (1988a, 1989). Suppose there are two technologies, A and B, available to a large market of potential adopters, both of which improve with the number of adoptions. Assume two types of adopters, R and S, each type equally prevalent, with 'natural' preferences for A and B respectively. Denote by $n_A(t)$ and $n_B(t)$ the number of agents adopting technology A or B at time t and suppose that each individual takes an irreversible decision about adoption. For each adopter type payoffs to adoption of A or B increase linearly with the number of previous adoptions, as is shown in Table 5.1.

The case $r = s = 0$ corresponds to constant returns and in this case agents R will always choose technology A, while agents S technology B. If $r > 0, s > 0$ there are increasing returns to adoption and one expects that in the long run one of the two technologies will become dominant in the market, although we need to have more information about the order of choices of agents R and S to predict which of the two technologies will prevail. Arthur injects randomness by assuming that the order of arrival of R and S types is unknown and that it is equally likely that an R or an S will arrive next to make his choice. Initially at

Table 5.1   Payoffs to adoption: linear increase with the number of previous adoptions

	Technology A	Technology B
agent R	$a_R + rn_A$	$b_R + rn_B$
agent S	$a_S + sn_A$	$b_S + sn_B$

with $a_R > b_R$ and $a_S < b_S$.

least, R agents will prefer A while S agents will prefer B; thus the difference in adoptions between A and B moves up or down by one unit with probability one half. However, if by chance a sufficient number of R-types cumulates, the payoffs of A will improve enough to cause future S-types to prefer to switch to A: from a given time onwards, both agent types choose the same technology A, with the result that technology A further increases its lead. Similarly, if a sufficient number of S-types cumulates, then B will improve sufficiently to cause R-types to switch to B, with the consequence that from a given time onwards everyone will choose B. These dynamics form a random walk with absorbing barriers on each side, the barriers corresponding to the lead in adoption it takes for each type to switch to the other alternative. Such barriers 'absorb' the process in the sense that once either is reached by random movement of the difference in adoptions between A and B, the process ceases to involve both technologies; that is, it becomes 'locked-in' to one technology only. This is an alternative way of saying that random walk theory guarantees that in this model absorption occurs eventually with probability one. Therefore, the adoption process is such that one of the two technologies will achieve a monopoly with certainty. Notice that this model exhibits the properties of multiple equilibria, possible inefficiency, lock-in, path-dependence and symmetry-breaking we discussed in Chapter 1, section 1.2.

In other papers Arthur, Ermoliev and Kaniovski (1983, 1985, 1987b) generalize this setting by considering K technologies instead of two, with more general payoffs-to-adoption functions, and keeping the assumption that the number of firms is continually increasing. It yields a generalized Polya urn model with unit adoptions which occur with probabilities influenced by past increments, and the analysis of the long-run proportions of firms using one technology is done applying the theorems we discussed in Chapter 2, section 2.7 to prove definite lock-in.

A number of studies have now used this technique (see, for example, David, 1987). The paper about industry location patterns by Arthur (1986) is an example which applies this technique to the dynamics of spatial-technology competitions. Here the theorems in Arthur, Ermoliev and Kaniovski (1985) are used to explain the fact that 'historical accidents' of early locational choice combined with subsequent economies of agglomeration can cause extreme regional concentrations of industry. Witt (1993) discusses these theorems in the context of rivalling institutions. Dosi and Kaniovski (1993) present three classes of examples using the method of generalized urn schemes in Arthur, Ermoliev and Kaniovski (1987a). In the first of them they assume that the adoption dynamics are driven by endogenous changes in the choices of risk-averse, imperfectly informed adopters. In the second example they consider an endogenous price dynamics of two alternative technologies driven by changes in their costs of production and/ or by the intertemporal behaviour of their producers. In the third example they consider an explicit spatial representation of the location of producers.

It has been pointed out that most results of this approach may be mitigated somewhat if some or all of the variants which are in the market initially are proprietary technology and 'sponsored' by foresighted firms. These firms will price strategically, taking early losses in order to establish their version as the dominant one, thereby allowing them to make larger profits later. Hanson's work (1985) provides the most complete analysis of such a model. The major distinction of this study from that of Arthur's is to make competition proprietary and to allow strategic pricing aimed at maximizing discounted expected profits in a market where heterogeneous adopters arrive at random. The competing technologies are incorporated into components produced by specific firms, which advance these alternative standards by strategically pricing the goods which utilize them. Hanson shows that for plausible assumptions on the peripheral makers cost and demand functions, a growth in the installed base of a system will lead to lower prices and more differentiation of offerings in the peripheral market. Moreover, he gives the conditions which lead current market shares to be strongly related to cumulative market shares, and using the theorems in Arthur, Ermoliev and Kaniovski (1985) he shows that monopoly by a single technology product is still a possible outcome. However, it is also possible that with weaker installed base effects or shorter effective time horizons, there will be no competitive exclusion and the market ends up shared. Unless very specific assumptions on the cost functions are introduced, it is unsolved whether the impact of foresight will make the systems evolve toward exclusion or not. Another contribution is by Habermeier (1989), which addresses the problem of expectations of future adoptions. He considers a rational expectations model with overlapping adopters to show that even with rational expectations, the long-term market outcome depends sensitively on the pattern of early chance events, and that only one variant of the technology will come to dominate the market in the long run, not necessarily the one which is socially optimal or most promising technically.

The model we discuss in this chapter represents another contribution to the field. In this chapter we will keep the basic structure of the Arthur's model and introduce another generalization. Our generalization follows from the remark that in Arthur's papers and in much of the literature following such an approach, with very few exceptions, there is a weakness: agents behave myopically. That is, they do not modify their expectations as the fortunes of alternatives change during the adoption process itself. In what follows we try instead to bring together the two features of increasing returns to adoption and non-myopic behaviour. In Arthur's model, randomness is introduced by lack of knowledge of the arrival sequence of the adopters who have natural preferences on different technologies. His model is developed within an equilibrium analysis. In our model, on the contrary, randomness enters in a homogeneous adopter-type setting because technological improvements occur in part by unpredictable breakthroughs. We study under what circumstances one technology can achieve a monopoly and eventually take the whole market, by formulating a firm's optimal decision problem. Our formulation of the decision problem takes into account the revision of the probabilities on the future states of the adoption process. This yields a version of the two-armed bandit problem.

The literature of statistical decision theory referring to two-armed bandit problems has stressed the possibility of ending up with a 'wrong' choice too. In the basic model of a two-armed bandit problem (Bellman, 1956) a decision-maker who follows optimal strategies will after an initial period of sampling settle on one arm and play it in preference to the other. However, the arm chosen will not necessarily be the correct one. Notice, incidentally, that the literature on two-armed bandit problems appears quite fragmentary and has rarely been applied by economists. Thus, this chapter also provides a link between the two views.

In this chapter we shall strenghten the results of the literature about lock-in with competing technologies with increasing returns to adoption. We shall show that by allowing the agent to learn in a Bayesian way, lock-in to inferior technologies is still possible. An early run of bad luck with a potentially superior technology may cause the decision-maker, perfectly rationally, to abandon it. Put it in another way, escape from inferior technological paths is not guaranteed. Moreover, the stronger the learning-by-doing, learning-by-using effects, the more likely it is that a 'wrong' technology is locked-in. That is to say, increasing returns have the role of strengthening the probability of getting to an inefficient result. We would like to stress that very similar results are obtained in Cowan (1991), with slightly different techniques.

Section 5.2 presents the model. Our central result is proved and discussed in sections 5.3 and 5.4. Finally, in section 5.5 some conclusions are drawn and a few policy implications of our findings are considered.

5.2. THE MODEL

Let us consider two 'unsponsored' technologies, A and B, which are available for performing the same task and are competing passively for a market. The term 'unsponsored', which was coined by Arthur, means that technologies do not compete strategically; that is they are not products that can be priced and manipulated, and therefore adoption of one technology displaces or precludes adoption of its rivals. There is one decision-maker who has to decide, each period, which technology to adopt. Randomness enters in this homogeneous adopter-type model because technological improvements occur in part by unpredictable breakthroughs. Moreover, as adoptions of A (or B) increase, learning-by-using and learning-by-doing effects take place and improved versions of A (or B) become available, with correspondingly higher payoffs or returns to the adopter. We shall suppose that the one-period returns to the two technologies A and B are described by the Table 5.2, where n_A and n_B denote the number of adoptions of A and B respectively.

Table 5.2   Payoffs to adoption: one period returns

A:	$H_A(n_A)$	with probability Π_A
	$L_A(n_A)$	with probability $1 - \Pi_A$
B:	$H_B(n_B)$	with probability Π_B
	$L_B(n_B)$	with probability $1 - \Pi_B$

and the following assumptions hold:

Assumption 1

$H_i(.)$ and $L_i(.)$ are continuous functions and are non-decreasing in $n_i, i = A, B$.

Assumption 2

For any $n_A = n_B = \bar{n}$ we have $H_A(\bar{n}) > H_B(\bar{n}) > L_B(\bar{n}) > L_A(\bar{n})$.

Assumption 3

Returns to adoption increase but are bounded:

$$\lim_{n_i \to \infty} H_i(n_i) = \bar{H}_i < \infty$$

$$\lim_{n_i \to \infty} L_i(n_i) = \bar{L}_i < \infty$$

$$i = A, B.$$

Assumption 1 is a central assumption. It means that there exist experience advantages. The more a technology is adopted, the more it is learned about it, and the higher the payoff becomes. Assumption 2 implies that technology B is less dispersed than technology A. For simplicity, we do not consider the case where H_A and H_B (and L_A and L_B) cross each other, although the analysis could be generalized to this case as well. Assumption 3 states that experience effects vanish, at least in infinite time.

With this formulation, two aspects of technological improvement can be captured. The 'endogenous' aspect of technological improvement, which is due to learning-by-doing and learning-by-using effects, is captured by the fact that as the number of adoptions increases, improved versions of the technologies become available and consequently the returns to adoptions become larger (Table 5.2 and Assumption 1). The 'exogenous' and uncertain aspect of technological change is captured by the fact that a 'high' payoff ($H_i(.)$ with probability Π_i) or a 'low' payoff ($L_i(.)$ with probability $1 - \Pi_i$) can result from uncertain breakthroughs, which cause variation in operating environments of the technologies (Table 5.2 and Assumption 2).

The decision-maker does not know the probabilities Π_A and Π_B with certainty. We assume that he possesses prior beliefs about Π_A and Π_B. He decides which technology to adopt at each stage after consulting his prior beliefs about Π_A and Π_B, and examining the record of 'high' payoffs (superscript H) and 'low' payoffs (superscript L) on the technologies so far.

5.2.1.   Preliminaries

Let us denote by

$$n_A^H, n_B^H (\text{ and } n_A^L, n_B^L)$$

the number of times that a 'high' payoff (or a 'low' payoff) is recorded for technology A and B respectively. Obviously, $n_B^H + n_A^L = n_A$ and $n_B^H + n_B^L = n_B$. We define the following statistics:

$$r_i = \frac{1}{n_i + 1}, \quad m_i = \frac{n_i^H}{n_i + 1}, \quad i = A, B.$$

The statistics r_i and m_i are sufficient statistics for the parameter Π_i; r_i is a statistic for the number of adoptions of technology i and m_i for the number of times that a 'high' payoff is recorded for technology i. Simple rules for updating m_i and r_i can be derived. If technology i is chosen, then m_i becomes $(m_i + r_i)/(1 + r_i)$ if a 'high' payoff is obtained, while it becomes $m_i/(1 + r_i)$ if a 'low' payoff is obtained. The information from the sample is contained in $(m, r) = (m_A, m_B, r_A, r_B)$ belonging to a fourfold copy of the closed interval [0, 1].

Given our assumption that the decision-maker does not know the parameters with certainty, we suppose that he possesses prior beliefs about the parameters summarized by a prior density function $g(\Pi_A, \Pi_B)$ such that $g(\Pi_A, \Pi_B) > 0$ for all $(\Pi_A, \Pi_B) \in [0, 1]^2$.

At each stage the most reliable estimate for Π_A and Π_B is given by the posterior mean of the decision-maker's beliefs about the values Π_A and Π_B, given the sample information (m, r) and the prior density $g(\Pi_A, \Pi_B)$. In particular, if experience gives (m, r), the prior beliefs will be updated from $g(\Pi_A, \Pi_B)$ to $j(\Pi_A, \Pi_B, m, r)$ according to Bayes' rule. Therefore the posterior mean of the decision-maker's belief about the value Π_i, given (m, r) and $g(\Pi_A, \Pi_B)$ is:

$$\lambda_i(m, r) = \int_0^1 \int_0^1 \Pi_i \, j(\Pi_A, \Pi_B, m, r) d\,\Pi_A d\,\Pi_B, \qquad i = A, B. \quad (5.1)$$

Notice that λ_i is the mean of a posterior distribution based on $n_i = (1 - r_i)/r_i$ observations. The function $\lambda_i(m, r)$ is defined and continuous for all (m, r) such that $r_i > 0, i = A, B$. It can be extended by continuity to $[0, 1]^4$ since $\lim_{r_i \to 0} \lambda_i(m, r) = m_i$. This follows from the fact that as $r_i \to 0$ the posterior distribution approaches a normal distribution with mean equal to the sample mean.

5.2.2. The Choice of Technologies

We assume that the decision-maker will choose the technology that maximizes the expected discounted value of his profits over an infinite horizon. Let δ be the discount factor, $0 < \delta < 1$. In order to compute the expected discounted value of the profits we will state the problem of the decision-maker as a dynamic programming problem.

$$\max_{y_t} E\left\{\sum_{t=0}^\infty \delta^t [y_t F_A \frac{(1 - r_A(t))}{r_A(t)} + (1 - y_t) F_B \frac{(1 - r_B(t))}{r_B(t)}\right\}$$

$$\text{subject to } y_t \in \{0, 1\} \quad (5.2)$$

and the sequential constraints that:

For $y_t = 1$

$$r_A(t) = r_A(t - 1)/(1 + r_A(t - 1))$$
$$r_B(t) = r_B(t - 1)$$

$$m_A(t) = \begin{cases} (m_A(t-1) + r_A(t-1))/(1 + r_A(t-1)), & \text{if 'high'} \\ m_A(t-1)/(1 + r_A(t-1)), & \text{if 'low'} \end{cases}$$

$$m_B(t) = m_B$$

$$F_A \frac{(1 - r_A(t))}{r_A(t)} = \begin{cases} H_A \dfrac{(1 - r_A(t))}{r_A(t)}, & \text{if 'high'} \\ L_A \dfrac{(1 - r_A(t))}{r_A(t)}, & \text{if 'low'} \end{cases}$$

For $y_t = 0$

$$r_B(t) = r_B(t-1)/(1 + r_B(t-1))$$

$$r_A(t) = r_A(t-1)$$

$$m_B(t) = \begin{cases} (m_B(t-1) + r_B(t-1))/(1 + r_B(t-1)), & \text{if 'high'} \\ m_B(t-1)/(1 + m_B(t-1)), & \text{if 'low'} \end{cases}$$

$$m_A(t) = m_A(t-1)$$

$$F_B \frac{(1 - r_B(t))}{r_B(t)} = \begin{cases} H_B \dfrac{(1 - r_B(t))}{r_B(t)} & \text{if 'high'} \\ L_B \dfrac{(1 - r_B(t))}{r_B(t)} & \text{if 'low'} \end{cases}$$

where $[1 - r_i(t)]/r_i(t)$ is the number of adoptions of i at time t. Obviously, $[1 - r_i(0)]/r_i(0) = 0, i = A, B$.

Let us explain the constraints above. If technology A is chosen at $t(y_t = 1)$, then m_B and r_B remain unchanged, while m_A and r_A change according to the rules explained in section 5.2.1. The value of the profits at t is given by $F_A((1 - r_A(t))/r_A(t))$, which can be either 'high' or 'low'. Analogous expressions hold if technology B is chosen at $t(y_t = 0)$.

Let

$$h_A(m, r) = (\frac{m_A + r_A}{1 + r_A}, m_B, \frac{r_A}{1 + r_A}, r_B);$$

$$l_A(m, r) = (\frac{m_A}{1 + r_A}, m_B, \frac{r_A}{1 + r_A}, r_B);$$

$$h_B(m, r) = (m_A, \frac{m_B + r_B}{1 + r_B}, r_A, \frac{r_B}{1 + r_B});$$

$$l_B(m,r) = (m_A, \frac{m_B}{1+r_B}, r_A, \frac{r_B}{1+r_B}).$$

Associated with (5.2) there is the functional equation:

$$W(m,r) = \max\{\lambda_A(m,r)[H_A(\frac{1-r_A}{r_A}) + \delta W(h_A(m,r)]$$

$$+(1-\lambda_A(m,r))[L_A(\frac{1-r_A}{r_A}) + \delta W(l_A(m,r))];$$

$$\lambda_B(m,r)[H_B(\frac{1-r_B}{r_B}) + \delta W(h_B(m,r))]$$

$$+(1-\lambda_B(m,r))[L_B(\frac{1-r_B}{r_B}) + \delta W(l_B(m,r))]\} \qquad (5.3)$$

which may be written as:

$$W(m,r) = \max_{i=A,B}\{V_i(m,r)\} \qquad (5.4)$$

where V is defined by:

$$V_i(m,r) = [\lambda_i(m,r)H_i(\frac{1-r_i}{r_i}) + (1-\lambda_i(m,r))L_i(\frac{1-r_i}{r_i})]$$

$$+ \delta\{\lambda_i(m,r)W(h_i(m,r)) + (1-\lambda_i(m,r))W(l_i(m,r))\}. (5.5)$$

Lemma

The functions $W(m,r)$ and $V(m,r)$ are continuous.

Proof

The proof is by an inductive argument. Let:

$$W_0(m,r) = 0$$

$$W^1(m,r) = \max_{i=A,B}\{V(m,r)\},$$

$$\text{where } V_i^1(m,r) = \lambda_i(m,r)H_i(\frac{1-r_i}{r_i}) + (1-\lambda_i(m,r))L_i(\frac{1-r_i}{r_i})$$

$$W^T(m,r) = \max_{i=A,B}\{V_i^T(m,r)\},$$

where $V_i^T(m,r) = \lambda_i(m,r)H_i(\dfrac{1-r_i}{r_i}) + (1 - \lambda_i(m,r))L_i(\dfrac{1-r_i}{r_i}) +$

$\delta\{\lambda_i(m,r)W^{T-1}(h_i(m,r)) + (1 - \lambda_i(m,r))W^{T-1}(l_i(m,r))\}.$

The Lemma can be proved through the following steps.

Step 1

The functions $W^T(m,r)$ and $V_i^T(m,r)$ are continuous.
Indeed the continuity of $\lambda_i(m,r)$, Assumption 1 and $W^0(m,r) = 0$ establish the property for $t = 1$. If we suppose that $V_i^{T-1}(m,r)$ and $W^{T-1}(m,r)$ are continuous then also $V_i^{T-1}(m,r)$ and $W^{T-1}(m,r)$ are because by the induction hypothesis they are sums of continuous functions.

Step 2

The functions $W^T(m,r)$ and $V_i^T(m,r)$ are monotonic in T.
Indeed, obviously $W^1(m,r) \geq W^0(m,r)$. If we assume that $W^{T-1}(m,r) \geq W^{T-2}(m,r)$, for every (m,r), then we get:

$$W^T(m,r) \geq \max\{\lambda_A(m,r)H_A(\dfrac{1-r_A}{r_A}) + (1 - \lambda_A(m,r))L_A(\dfrac{1-r_A}{r_A})$$
$$+ \delta[\lambda_A(m,r)W^{T-2}(h_A(m,r)) + (1 - \lambda_A(m,r))W^{T-2}(l_A(m,r))];$$
$$\lambda_B(m,r)H_B(\dfrac{1-r_B}{r_B}) + (1 - \lambda_B(m,r))L_B(\dfrac{1-r_B}{r_B})$$
$$+ \delta[\lambda_B(m,r)W^{T-2}(h_B(m,r))$$
$$+ (1 - \lambda_B(m,r))W^{T-2}(l_B(m,r))]\} = W^{T-1}(m,r).$$

Since $W^T(m,r)$ is monotonic in T, also $V_i^T(m,r)$ is.

Step 3

The sequences $\{W^T(m,r)\}$ and $\{V_i^T(m,r)\}$ are bounded above and converge.
Indeed, consider $\max\{\bar{H}_A, \bar{L}_A, \bar{H}_B, \bar{L}_B\} = \bar{H}_A$. For $0 < \delta < 1$ it follows that $\bar{H}_A/(1 - \delta)$ is a finite number. Obviously, $W^0(m,r) =$

$0 < \bar{H}_A/(1 - \delta)$. Moreover $W^1(m,r) \leq \bar{H}_A < \bar{H}_A/(1 - \delta)$. If we assume that $W^{T-1}(m,r) \leq \bar{H}_A/(1 - \delta)$ then it follows:

$$W^T(m,r) \leq \max\{\lambda_A(m,r)H_A(\frac{1 - r_A}{r_A}) + (1 - \lambda_A(m,r))L_A(\frac{1 - r_A}{r_A})$$

$$+ \delta\bar{H}_A/(1 - \delta); \lambda_B(m,r)H_B(\frac{1 - r_B}{r_B}) + (1 - \lambda_B(m,r))L_B(\frac{1 - r_B}{r_B})$$

$$+ \delta\bar{H}_A/(1 - \delta)\} = W^1(m,r) + \delta\bar{H}_A/(1 - \delta) \leq \bar{H}_A$$

$$+ \delta\bar{H}_A/(1 - \delta) = \bar{H}_A/(1 - \delta).$$

Since $W^T(m,r)$ is monotonic in T and bounded above, then the sequence $W^T(m,r)$ converges. The same is true for $V_i^T(m,r)$.

Step 4

The functions $W^T(m,r)$ and $V_i^T(m,r)$ converge uniformly to $W(m,r)$ and $V_i(m,r)$. Indeed, the following inequality clearly holds: $W(m,r) \leq W^T(m,r) + \delta^T\bar{H}_A/(1 - \delta)$, and therefore $|W(m,r) - W^T(m,r)| \leq \delta^T\bar{H}_A/(1 - \delta)$. Since this inequality is independent of (m,r), then uniform convergence is established. An immediate consequence is that $W(m,r)$ and $V_i(m,r)$ are continuous.

Let $Z_B = \{(m,r) \in (0,1)^4; V_B(m,r) > V_A(m,r)\}$. The principle of optimality states that an optimal policy for this problem is to choose technology B whenever (m,r) belongs to Z_B. Since $V_A(m,r)$ and $V_B(m,r)$ are continuous then Z_B is an open set.

5.3. WHEN DOES TECHNOLOGY *B* ACHIEVE A MONOPOLY?

The following result establishes up to which point the choice of technology A is not convenient.

Proposition 5.1

For every Π_B' such that $\Pi_B > \Pi_B' > 0$ there exist $\varepsilon_1 > 0, \varepsilon_2 > 0, \bar{\delta} > 0$ such that $V_B(m,r) > V_A(m,r)$ whenever $m_A + r_A < \varepsilon_1$, $r_B < \varepsilon_2$, $m_B \geq \Pi_B - \Pi_B' > 0$, and $0 < \delta < \bar{\delta}$.

Proof

The proof consists of two steps.

Step 1

Consider $K = \{(m,r) \in (0,1)^4; m_A = r_A = 0, m_B \geq \Pi_B - \Pi_B' > 0$ and $r_B < \varepsilon_2\}$, which is a compact set. Consider $Z_B = \{(m,r) \in (0,1)^4; V_B(m,r) > V_A(m,r)\}$. We want to show the conditions under which $K \subset Z_B$. Consider:

$$V_B(0, m_B, 0, r_B) = \lambda_B(0, m_B, 0, r_B) H_B(\frac{1 - r_B}{r_B})$$
$$+ (1 - \lambda_B(0, m_B, 0, r_B)) L_B(\frac{1 - r_B}{r_B}) + \delta\{\lambda_B(0, m_B, 0, r_B) W(h(m_B))$$
$$+ (1 - \lambda_B(0, m_B, 0, r_B)) W(l_B(m_B))\} > L_B(\frac{1 - r_B}{r_B}).$$

The last inequality holds under Assumption 2.
Suppose now that

$$V_B(0, m_B, 0, r_B) \leq V_A(0, m_B, 0, r_B).$$

In this case

$$W(0, m_B, 0, r_B) = V_A(0, m_B, 0, r_B) = \bar{L}_A + \delta W(0, m_B, 0, r_B)$$

because $\lambda_A(0, m_B, 0, r_B) = m_A = 0$ if $r \to 0$; that is, $V_A(0, m_B, 0, r_B) = \bar{L}_A/(1 - \delta)$, which is a contradiction if $L_B((1 - r_B)/r_B) > \bar{L}_A/(1 - \delta)$, that is if $\delta < \bar{\bar{\delta}} = 1 - \bar{L}_A/L_B((1 - r_B)/r_B)$. Notice that $\bar{\bar{\delta}} > 0$ if r_B is sufficiently small, say if $r_B < \varepsilon_2$. Therefore, if $\delta < \bar{\bar{\delta}}$ then $V_B(0, m_B, 0, r_B) > V_A(0, m_B, 0, r_B)$.

Step 2

Since Z_B is open, then for each $(0, m_B, 0, r_B) \in K$ there is a suitable ball (in the max norm) centered at $(0, m_B, 0, r_B)$ which is contained in Z_B. Since K is compact we can find a finite collection of such balls covering K, that is

$$K \subset \bigcup_{j \in J} B_j,$$

where J is a finite set. Let ε_1 be the minimum radius of the B_js with $j \in J$. Then consider:

$$K^{\varepsilon_1} = \{(m,r) \in (0,1)^4; m_A + r_A < \varepsilon_1, m_B \geq \Pi_B - \Pi'_B > 0$$
$$\text{and } r_B < \varepsilon_2\}$$

Notice that every $(m,r) \in K^{\varepsilon_1}$ belongs to some B_j for a suitable $j \in J$. Hence

$$\max\{|m_A|, |m_B - m_B^j|, |r_A|, |r_B - r_B^j|\} \leq \varepsilon_{1j},$$

for any $(m,r) \in K^{\varepsilon_1}$, where ε_{1j} is the radius of B_j. Thus we get $K^{\varepsilon_1} \subset Z_B$.

In Proposition 5.1 the expressions:

$$m_A + r_A < \varepsilon_1, \text{and } r_B < \varepsilon_2, m_B \geq \Pi_B - \Pi'_B > 0 \qquad (5.6)$$

give an exact specification of what is meant by 'sufficiently bad' experience on technology A and 'sufficiently good' experience on technology B. Indeed, they imply that the decision-maker is sufficiently sure that adopting technology A will not yield 'high' profits, since the statistics for the number of times that a 'high' profit is recorded for technology A after a large number of adoptions is sufficiently small $(m_A + r_A < \varepsilon_1)$; and that the decision-maker thinks it sufficiently likely that adopting technology B will yield 'high' profits, because the statistics for the number of times that a 'high' profit is recorded for technology B after a large number of adoptions is strictly positive $(m_B \geq \Pi_B - \Pi_{B'} > 0$ and $r_B < \varepsilon_2)$.

Then Proposition 5.1 can be interpreted as follows. If the decision-maker observes that after a certain number of sequences on A and B experience on technology A is sufficiently poor while it is sufficiently good on B, then, for appropriate values of the discount factor δ, it is more profitable to choose B rather than A. To complete the proof, we need to show that it is possible that experience on technology B is not so erratic that the decision-maker will never choose technology A again. Actually we can prove the following:

Proposition 5.2

A decision-maker who follows an optimal strategy will with positive probability choose technology B infinitely often and A only a finite number of times.

Proof

A proof can be given which follows the argument in Rothschild (1974a, pp. 197–8).

5.4. LOCK-IN TO THE 'WRONG' TECHNOLOGY

The results we have obtained in the section 5.3 make no use of the relation between the true probabilities Π_A and Π_B. In particular, nothing in Proposition 5.1 and Proposition 5.2 guarantees that technology B is the more efficient one, that is, the technology the decision-maker would have chosen had he or she known the exact sequence of 'high' and 'low' payoffs. As a consequence, the market may be locked-in to the 'wrong' technology.

In our model there are two distinct elements driving the system to lock in to one technology (see also Cowan, 1991). One is the reduction of uncertainty. When the adoption process begins the returns of the technologies are uncertain, but early use of them reduces such uncertainty. This effect will, by itself, cause lock-in to occur, and is indeed what happens in the simple two-armed bandit model.

The 'wrong' technology result can be due to initial priors or bad luck with the first implementations of the superior technology. Because of this, the 'wrong' technology can then be chosen, and if it does not have very bad luck it will continue to be chosen; on the other side, the other technology, not being used, has no way to demonstrate its superiority and therefore the market becomes locked-in to the inferior alternative.

In our model there is also another element driving lock-in; that is, the presence of increasing returns which have an effect on the probability of locking into a 'wrong' technology. In particular, the lock-in result occurs more quickly, the stronger the increasing returns to adoption. Let us give the following:

Definition

Compare the two pairs of returns to adoption for technology i $(H_i(n_i), L_i(n_i))$ and $(H_i{}^*(n_i), L_i{}^*(n_i))$. If $H_i(n_i) > H_i{}^*(n_i)$ and $L_i{}^*(n_i) \geq L_i{}^*(n_i), An_i$, or $H_i(n_i) \geq H_i{}^*(n_i)$ and $L_i(n_i) > L_i{}^*(n_i), An_i$, then we say that the learning-by-doing and learning-by-using effects are stronger in the first case than in the second.

The following result holds:

Proposition 5.3

The stronger the learning-by-doing and learning-by-using effects, the more likely it is that the 'wrong' technology is locked-in.

Proof

Following Whittle (1981, 1988) we can construct a dynamic allocation index (DAI) for each technology i, $i = A, B$. The index is defined as follows. Consider a modification of the above two-armed bandit process, which allows the additional option of choosing a known technology, for which the probability of getting a payoff of value 1 is p, and the probability of getting 0 is $(1 - p)$ (standard bandit process). Let

$$M = \Sigma_{t=0}^{\infty} \delta^t p = p/(1 - \delta).$$

Now offer the decision-maker the choice between choosing the known technology forever, or choosing technology i, $i = A, B$, at least once and possibly more times, with the option of switching at some future time to the known one, which must then be chosen forever. The value of p for which the decision-maker is indifferent between these two options is the value of the DAI for technology i. The DAI policy consists in choosing each period the technology which has the highest index value. Let $\varphi_i = \max[M, L_i \varphi_i]$, where:

$$L_i \varphi_i(m, r) = \lambda_i(m, r) H_i \left(\frac{1 - r_i}{r_i}\right) + (1 - \lambda_i(m, r)) L_i \left(\frac{1 - r_i}{r_i}\right)$$
$$+ \delta \{\lambda_i(m, r) \varphi_i(h_i(m, r)) + (1 - \lambda_i(m, r)) \varphi_i(l_i(m, r))\}$$

that is, φ_i is the maximal expected reward for the modified process we have described above. The DAI is defined by $M = \varphi_i(m, r)$; that is, the options between continuation with technology i or retirement with reward M must be indifferent. This implies that $M = L_i\varphi_i(m, r)$. Because of the presence of increasing returns to adoption we get $L_i\varphi i \geq M$, and therefore continuation is always optimal. It follows that

$$M = \sum_{t=0}^{\infty}\delta^t[\lambda_i(m(t), r(t))H_i(\frac{1 - r_i(t)}{r_i(t)})$$
$$+ (1 - \lambda_i(m(t), r(t)))L_i(\frac{1 - r_i(t)}{r_i(t)})]$$

and therefore we get the following DAI for technology i:

$$p = (1 - \delta)\sum_{t=0}^{\infty}\delta^t[\lambda_i(m(t), r(t))H_i(\frac{1 - r_i(t)}{r_i(t)})$$
$$+ (1 - \lambda_i(m(t), r(t)))L_i(\frac{1 - r_i(t)}{r_i(t)})]. \qquad (5.7)$$

From (5.7) it follows that p increases with the degree of increasing returns to adoption because the expression within square brackets increases. As a result, suppose that the 'wrong' technology was used until it had a large lead in learning (see also Cowan, 1991). The stronger the learning-by-doing and learning-by-using effects, the larger p, the easier it is to gain this lead. Even if the estimates of the other technology are accurate, an erroneously high estimate of the 'wrong' technology will allow it to be used, and increasing returns will allow it to continue being used. This implies that strong increasing returns have the role of strengthening the probability of getting to an inferior technology.

5.5. SOME POLICY ISSUES

We have shown that increasing returns can cause the economy gradually to lock itself into an outcome not necessarily superior to alternatives, even though the decision-maker is allowed to learn in a Bayesian way.

This finding can be relevant for policy implications too. Where a central authority with full information on future returns to alternative adoption paths knows which technology has superior long-run potential, it can attempt to make the market adopt this technology. When there are increasing returns to adoption, in David's phrase (1987), there are only 'narrow windows' in time, during which effective public policy interventions can be made at moderate resource costs. But if it is not clear in advance which technologies have most potential promise, then the central authority intervention is even more problematic. As it is shown above, 'an early run of bad luck with a potentially superior technology may cause the central authority, perfectly rational, to abandon it' (Arthur, 1988b). The implication is that even with central control, escape from 'wrong' technologies is not guaranteed.

David (1987) has stressed a few problem areas for policy-makers when positive feedbacks are present in adoption processes and has affixed colourful labels to some of them: the 'narrow policy window paradox', the 'blind giant's quandary' and the 'angry orphans' problem'. Policy interventions involve the manipulation of technology adoption by means of taxes and/or subsidies, or informational programmes and announcements designed to shape expectations about the future adoption decisions of other agents. When there are increasing returns to adoption such interventions tend to be confined towards the very beginning of the dynamic process and, in addition, have an uncertain and usually brief temporal duration. In other words, there are 'narrow policy windows' for effective public intervention. Essentially, this is due to the fact that the flow of new adopters in the market is variable and not known precisely, so that it is difficult to predict when the global market shares will reach the boundary values that cause lock-in or lock-out among competing technologies. On the contrary, at the very beginning of the diffusion process there are few adopters and the increasing returns effects play a less dominant role in sequential decisions, so that intervention is easier. However, a further dilemma arises: public agencies are likely to be at their most powerful in exercising influence upon future adoptions just when they know least about what should be done. That is, they are just like 'blind giants' and yet a passive 'wait and see' attitude on the part of public agencies is not necessarily what is called for in a state of uncertainty. More sophisticated policies are needed for an inadequately informed public agent in order to prevent the 'narrow window' from slamming shut before the policy-makers are better able to perceive their relevant future options.

In addition to these problems, there may difficulties created by angry technological 'orphans'; that is, the losers of the technological competition who can complain publicly that their technological expectations were falsely nourished by governmental programmes and may form lobbies and pressure groups to protect themselves against public intervention. At the same time, it may sometimes be desirable as a policy option to keep more than one technology on the market to avoid monopoly problems or to retain 'requisite variety' as a hedge against future changes in the economic environment. It is apparent from these remarks that the question of using well-timed subsidies to prevent the adoption process from locking-in and locking-out technologies has not a definite answer. It is even more complex if one accepts the view that there is a coevolution of technologies, organizations and institutions (David, 1994), because the resulting self-reinforcing mechanisms make it more difficult to think of an effective intervention aiming at stabilizing such an unstable dynamic process.

Further policy issues have been raised by other contributions analyzing oligopolistic industries in the presence of learning-by-doing and in particular how learning affects market structures (see for example, Agliardi, 1990, 1992b; Dasgupta and Stiglitz, 1988b; Fudenberg and Tirole, 1983; Ghemawat and Spence, 1985; Mookherjee and Ray, 1989, 1991; Spence, 1981). Most of these papers, which follow a different approach from this chapter, stress that when learning possibilities are powerful, unless spillovers among firms are perfect, there is a tendency towards the emergence of dominant firms and thus concentration. For example, Dasgupta and Stiglitz (1988) show that if the scope of learning is large, an initial cost advantage accumulates over time so that market share increases for the advantaged firm, possibly leading to monopoly. In Agliardi (1990) we study a similar problem with a different form of asymmetries, to show that a firm which has an initial cost disadvantage may become the advantaged one in a subsequent period because of learning effects. Then we study a case of asymmetric information and examine whether learning effects reduce the prospects for profitable collusion in a dynamic game (Agliardi, 1992b). We show that it does not follow that a single large firm in an industry must *per se* be bad. If learning effects are significant, monopoly is not necessarily the worst form of market structure: duopoly may be worse for society, the infant phase of an industry may be prolonged. Moreover, during the learning phase a protected private monopolist may wish to price its product below its current unit production cost. However, if an incumbent firm does not price its product below production costs it does not follow that it is engaged in predatory pricing. The main conclusion we can draw from these considerations is that the common attitude in policy interventions, and especially anti-trust policies, may be questionable in the presence of learning effects.

Finally, a last remark is in order. We observe that the intriguing point of much of the analysis of this chapter comes from the fact that the number of firms is continually increasing in this setting, and this gives qualitatively different results from the fixed population urn model we used in Chapter 4. In modelling technological change it is by no means clear whether the assumption of a fixed number of firms adopting different technologies, or being replaced by new firms, is better than that of an arbitrarily growing number of firms: which model is chosen has certainly important consequences for the nature of the results. Moreover, it should be emphasized that the set of technologies available could expand over time. This would add considerably to the analytical complications but also represent a meaningful area of future research.

6 Regularities in the Aggregate Behaviour of Interacting Economic Agents

6.1. SOME CONDITIONS FOR THE EMERGENCE OF INSTITUTIONS

There are situations in which agents' behaviour or agents' choices depend on the behaviour or the choices of other agents. In these cases we have to look at the system of interactions between individuals and their environment. Schelling (1978) provides examples of such interactive behaviour. People distribute themselves and congregate at parties and receptions, or form crowds at a rally, a riot or a spectacle, without following a single mode of behaviour. Sometimes people want to be close, sometimes spread out; the people on the edge of a crowd may be pushing to get in and the people in the middle are being crushed. The best and commonest examples are from everyday life. People get separated and integrated by sex, race, age, language, social status or by patterns of acquaintance and friendship. Age at marriage and age differences between spouses are affected by the ages at which others marry. Divorce and the prospects of remarriage depend on whether there is a high rate of turnover in particular age brackets. What other people in the same area are doing heavily influences other kind of behaviours such as the choice of the language, the diffusion of rumour, gossip and news, information and misinformation. The same kind of factor explains the formation of mobs and riots, panic behaviour, rules of the road, taste, style and fashion.

Such interactions can be found in many diverse economic situations: in the processes that involve 'contagion', 'mimicking' or 'herding', that have been studied in the literature on financial crises and bubbles in financial markets; in the choice of technologies and diffusion of technological standards when there are 'network externalities' and sufficiently low switching costs; within models of the 'economics of conformism', 'threshold' behaviour and 'critical mass' models, where the pressure to conform can be driven by direct economic consequences, for example because of strong complementarities, or by purely social effects, such as reputation or the feeling of belonging to a group.

These examples highlight the important role played by the pressure to conform and, more generally, show how important it is to understand individual decision-making of interacting agents in an environment characterized by positive feedbacks to explain regularities at the aggregate level. The purpose of this chapter is to provide a framework to analyze these kinds of decision-making as well as their implications. The basic idea underlying the approach in this chapter is that by taking account of the interaction between individual agents we may get interesting behaviour at the aggregate level. Individuals may be influenced by each other's choices, expectations, or simply interact with certain agents. Interactions may be deterministic or stochastic, as may the underlying communication network itself. Thus there can be a deterministic set of links used in a random way or the links can themselves be stochastic. Such a view leads us to put forward an equilibrium theory which is strongly affected by the information available to agents, their mode of learning about their economic environment, the process of beliefs formation and the evolution of interactions among agents, and all this is determined by the particular path followed in the economy. Knowledge or information, and the way it can be processed, disseminated and then affect individuals' actions, is the means by which irreversibilities are generated in the economy. Thus, in this framework 'history matters' because the equilibrium outcome will be history-dependent.

These elements can be relevant to studying the emergence of institutions. In abstract terms, institutions can be defined as orderly and more or less persistent behaviour patterns, rules or set of rules that constrain or govern organized patterns of behaviours' (North, 1990). Social norms and institutions are devices that give structure or order to social situations. They do this by giving all of the agents in a particular situation an idea of what type of behaviour they can expect from each other, and they act upon this information. In some instances institutions supplement competitive markets, in other circumstances they totally replace them. Some of the institutions are explicitly agreed to and codified into law; others are only tacitly agreed to and evolve endogenously from the attempts of the individuals to maximize their objective functions. Some lead to optimal social outcomes. In any case, they prescribe the type of behaviour that is acceptable in specific situations. More precisely, Lesourne (1992) characterizes the emergence of institutions in the following way, in addition to the case in which an institution is imposed on a market exogenously: the formation of rules of behaviour and regularities in the form of conventions; the emergence of new agents or group of agents of a different category from those existing previously, or coalitions of existing agents which originate as a result of cooperative processes; creation of new markets induced by the dynamics of the economic system, although in this case the new institutions can be of the same nature of those existing originally.

In the examples at the beginning of this section we listed problems in which agents pass on to their successors a wide variety of social rules of thumb, institutions, norms and conventions that facilitate coordination of economic and social activities. Although social institutions are predominantly concerned with solving social coordination problems, there are cases in which anti-coordination or conflict of interest between agents is more relevant. In this sense, the class of social institutions is broader than the class of social conventions and this is true also in terms of the mechanisms necessary to enforce them. Indeed, as Schotter (1981) states, institutions are not necessarily self-policing and may sometimes require some external authority, such as the state, to enforce them.

In this chapter we shall discuss a few approaches in the literature to the aggregate behaviour of interacting economic agents, with particular relevance to coordination problems and coordination institutions. This chapter is less homogeneous than the previous chapters, both in terms of the economic applications, which are not necessarily about technological choices, and in terms of the techniques and the variety of models we consider. The literature on this subject is sparse and we are still very far from having a theory about the role of economic institutions and social norms. Our attempt in this chapter is to provide at least a unifying framework to analyze the evolution of aggregate behaviour. Our view is that by incorporating how agents interact in our models we enrich the types of aggregate behaviour that can occur. For this reason we believe that the work discussed in this chapter may represent a further step in the direction of thinking of the economy as a self-organized system.

The chapter is organized as follows. In sections 6.2 – 6.5 we mainly deal with conventions and discuss evolution in games, models of 'herd behaviour', where there is some externality generated by the choices made by the members of the population, dynamic models of local interaction. Then in section 6.6 we shall present a model of morphogenesis.

6.2. THE EVOLUTION OF CONVENTIONS

A convention is a 'regularity in behaviour which is agreed to by all members of a society and which specifies behaviour in the specific recurrent situations' (Schotter, 1981). The notion can be best understood with a coordination game, which is defined by the following payoff matrix:

$$
\begin{array}{ccc}
 & s_1 & s_2 \\
s_1 & a,a & b,c \\
s_2 & c,b & d,d
\end{array}
$$

where $a > c$ and $d > b$. Here there is no conflict of interest; nevertheless, in spite of convergence of preferences, the coordination between participants is not trivial, because two solutions are possible: indeed, there are two strict Nash equilibria, that is $E_1 = (s_1, s_1)$ and $E_2 = (s_2, s_2)$. The point has been thoroughly discussed by Schelling (1960), who proposed the use of 'focal points' to achieve coordination. The riskiness of s_1 relative to s_2 is also relevant here.

A convention is self-sustaining: each agent will choose to follow it provided they expect the others to follow it. Everyone conforms, everyone expects others to conform and everyone wants to conform given that everyone else conforms. It is an equilibrium that everyone expects. The question which arises is the following: how do expectations become established when there is more than one equilibrium?

Indeed, one essential aspect of conventions is the self-reinforcing one. When one considers the case of a game with N players, rather than just two players, this means that, if there exists a small number of agents who do not conform to the convention, they will obtain a payoff which is smaller than what they would have obtained by following the convention. This follows from the fact that in this kind of coordination games the payoff from the choice of a strategy is an increasing function of the number of individuals choosing that strategy.

The role played by conformity effects and focal point processes in the emergence and stability of conventions does not ensure their Pareto efficiency. In the examples above, if $a > d$, then $E_1 = (s_1, s_1)$ Pareto dominates $E_2 = (s_2, s_2)$. It is easy to find situations in which the established convention is inefficient. The standardization of complementary products provides many examples of conventions. David's (1985) analysis of the QWERTY keyboard which we discussed in Chapter 5 is an example of inefficient convention. Moreover, one can note that subjects participating in experiments on a class of coordination games under conditions of 'strategic uncertainty' frequently do not succeed in coordinating on the Pareto dominant equilibrium (van Huyck, Battalio and Beil, 1990). By 'strategic uncertainty' we mean that even if players have complete information, they can be expected to be uncertain about how other players will respond when there is more than one equilibrium. In these experiments, several examples of coordination failure were indicated. In fact, they revealed a systematic discrimination between strict Nash equilibria that appear to be driven by the presence of uncertainty about which equilibrium strategy other decision-makers will choose. Put another way, some subjects conclude that it is too risky to choose the payoff dominant action and most subjects focus on more secure outcomes. This implies that the selection principle can be based on the riskiness of an equilibrium point. As a consequence, in order for individuals to coordinate themselves efficiently, they should be able to overcome 'strategic uncertainty' in some way.

One approach pursuing this aim appears in the literature that received a strong impetus from Harsanyi and Selten's (1988) book, where solutions to the selection problem are derived from a clear understanding of individual decision-making (Carlsson and van Damme, 1993a, 1993b; Crawford, 1991). To use Binmore's (1987) terminology, such an approach remains in the eductive context: the situations are represented by a game that is played only once, where players are superrational and can reason themselves towards equilibria. The approach in Carlsson and van Damme (1993a, 1993b) is based on the idea that the payoff parameters of a game can be observed only with some noise. They consider Stag Hunt Games, that is, N-person symmetric binary choice games, where each player can play either a safe strategy that yields a certain payoff irrespective of what the opponents do, or a risky strategy that yields a payoff that increases monotonically with the number of players that follow this strategy. All data in these games are common knowledge, except for the payoff associated with the safe action. They assume that each player receives a signal that provides an unbiased estimate of the unknown payoff, but the signals are noisy so that the true value of such payoff will not be common knowledge. As a result, this creates an incomplete information game – to be called a global game – which is based on a perturbation of the players' payoff information of the original game. The question addressed in this context is which choice is rational at each signal in the perturbed game. It is shown that the global game is almost dominance solvable: for all but a small set of parameter values unique iteratively dominant actions exist. In particular, by playing these dominant strategies, players coordinate on the risk dominant equilibrium of the actual game that was selected by chance. The argument driving this result is lack of common knowledge. Although in the perturbed game each player has a precise enough knowledge about the unknown payoff once each of them receives a given signal, there is no common knowledge about such payoff among players. The lack of common knowledge forces the players to take a global perspective in solving the perturbed game: the idea is that as long as player i thinks that some player j may think that some player k may think that. . . some player l plays a given dominant strategy in the actual game, then player i will play the same strategy himself.

In Agliardi (1995) we analyze the process by which information is transmitted and thus can affect individuals' decisions and the equilibrium selection, by means of an example in a class of multiperson coordination games with the characteristics of the discussion above. We distinguish between games where agents move simultaneously and games where agents move sequentially. In simultaneous move games the structure is a Stag Hunt Game and there is an 'infection' argument based on how players infer each others' actions. In the sequential move game agents can observe the moves of the others before, so that a pure 'infection' argument does not hold, and 'informational cascades' may eventually emerge; that is, situations in which an individual's action does not depend on his private information signal (Bikhchandani, Hirshleifer and Welch, 1992; In Ho Lee, 1993). In particular, we show that there is a positive probability that a 'cascade' is 'wrong'; that is, agents take a given action when the correct action would have been a different one. As a result, the order of moves is a crucial element for the prediction of the equilibrium outcome in this kind of game. In particular, while in the simultaneous move game it is lack of common knowledge that drives the equilibrium outcome, in the sequential move game there is a problem of aggregation of information of numerous individuals. Ideally, if the information of many previous individuals is aggregated, later individuals should converge to the correct action. However, once a 'cascade' has started, actions convey no information about private signals; thus an individual's action does not improve later decisions. That is to say, the agent who takes an action has a finer information set and a different posterior which cannot be transmitted to others through the action choice.

6.3. EVOLUTIONARY GAME DYNAMICS

A substantial literature has developed recently, concerning the evolution of conventions within evolutionary game theory, in the context of societal games played by randomly formed group of players (Ellison, 1993; Foster and Young, 1990; Friedman, 1991; Kandori, Mailath and Rob, 1993; Mailath, 1993; Young, 1993). The crucial role in these models is given by perpetual perturbations, which yield very different results from models with one-time perturbations. Related studies of evolutionary dynamics include Ellison and Fudenberg (1993), Fudenberg and Harris (1992) and Samuelson (1993), among many others.

   Evolutionary game theory has provided a fairly complete account of issues such as asymptotic properties and equilibrium selection for a large class of games that includes coordination games and common interest games. To fix ideas, let us consider the following symmetric game, taken from Mailath (1993):

$$
\begin{array}{c c c}
 & X & Y \\
X & 3,3 & 4,0 \\
Y & 0,4 & 5,5
\end{array}
$$

In this game $E_1 = (X, X)$ is the risk-dominant equilibrium, while $E_2 = (Y, Y)$ is the Pareto dominant equilibrium. Mailath (1993) describes an evolutionary model in which a finite population is repeatedly matched to play the game, with strategy choices driven by a best response dynamics (adaptive dynamics) and perturbed by rare *mutations*. As the probability of a mutation approaches zero, the limiting distribution of this model becomes concentrated at the risk dominant equilibrium. To see why this occurs, notice that the best reply dynamics continually push the system to either the state in which all agents play X or all agents play Y. A switch from one of these states to the other can occur only if a wave of simultaneous mutations changes sufficiently many agents from the prevailing strategy to the other, making the latter a best reply. In the limit, as the probability of a mutation becomes small, the ergodic distribution of the Markov process will concentrate all of its probability on the equilibrium that is hardest to escape, which will be the equilibrium that takes more mutations to escape. This is at the risk dominant equilibrium, since by definition this equilibrium has the larger basin of attraction under best reply dynamics.

Notice that this result is obtained without giving any explanation of how expectations are formed, and the process by which information is transmitted and thus can affect individuals' decisions and equilibrium selection is not spelled out in this approach.

Indeed, a standard evolutionary model consists of the following elements: a set of players; their strategy space; a payoff matrix; a *matching technology* that describes the interaction between players; a specification for the *replicator dynamics* which determines the growth rate of the population that is using a given strategy; some form of experimentation or *mutations*, that is, there is a small probability that agents change their strategies at random. Most evolutionary models assume that individual players are *myopic* and cannot influence the social outcome, so that there is no strategic effect to take into account. Some form of *inertia* is usually introduced; that is, not all agents react instantaneously to their environment. Moreover, populations are usually finite and players are randomly matched before each play of the game.

The dynamics for evolutionary models with finite populations are typically path-dependent. With a finite number of players, even when there is random matching, the experience of every player depends on the pure strategies played by each of his opponents: as a consequence, play becomes obviously correlated. A large but finite number of agents does not, in general, eliminate path-dependence. Kandori, Mailath and Rob (1993) assume, in addition to constant inertia and experimentation (or mutation) rates, a complete matching of the players, which makes their model stationary Markovian. With mutations it is clear that the system perpetually fluctuates between the equilibria. The interesting thing is that upsetting an equilibrium is more difficult the more mutations are required to escape from its basin of attraction. This implies that the system spends most of the time at the equilibrium which is more difficult to upset, when the mutation rate is small. In the Kandori, Malaith and Rob model, the equilibrium which is selected is the risk dominant, which has a larger basin of attraction. Indeed more mistakes are required to pull the system away from the risk dominant equilibrium than are necessary to pull it away from any other equilibrium. Hence, as the noise vanishes, the risk dominant equilibrium becomes infinitely more likely than any other equilibrium, and therefore any other configuration of play.

In a different way, Young (1993) modifies the best reply selection dynamics by assuming that agents have finite memory and that they play best replies to random samples from their finite past histories, which introduces inertia into the model and suppress the sources of path-dependence, making their model stationary Markovian. Indeed, this device introduces sufficient randomness into the selection dynamics to guarantee that, for a large class of games, the selection dynamics will themselves necessarily converge on a strict equilibrium. Extending the argument of Kandori, Mailath and Rob, Young then describes an algorithm to identify the stochastically stable states of general games. The concept of stochastically stable states is that of a state that is restored repeatedly when the evolutionary process is constantly buffeted by small random shocks. In Young (1993) the intuition that in the limit equilibria which require more mistakes to be left by the system will be infinitely more likely than others is still valid, but the details become intricate indeed.

Foster and Young (1990) first introduced the concept of stochastically stable states in evolutionary models. They consider a model with a continuum of agents and study the replicator dynamics in continuous time, assuming that the population shares are perturbed by a Brownian motion. A closely related model in continuous time and space is that of Fudenberg and Harris (1992), who introduce aggregate shocks, perturbing the size of the population playing a strategy directly. This yields a process that is not ergodic and with quite different properties from that of Foster and Young (1990).

Most of the above-mentioned models make some important qualitative predictions about the evolution of conventions. For example, even if we know the initial state of society, we cannot predict what the prevailing convention will be in the future: societies with very similar initial conditions may turn out to be operating very different conventions; that is, processes are path-dependent. However, lock-in is excluded whenever repeated stochastic shocks to the system are allowed, and so a society may flip from one convention to another. In particular, Young (1996) distinguishes between a local conformity effect and a global diversity effect. Kandori, Mailath, Rob (1993) and Young (1993) show that if all agents have a positive probability of interacting, if they have sufficiently incomplete information, and if random deviations have sufficiently low probability, then most of the time most of the population will be using the same convention; that is, there will be a local conformity effect. Now compare two societies that are alike in every way except that they do not communicate with one another, and run the process separately in each, starting from similar initial conditions. It can be shown that at any sufficiently distant future time there is a positive probability that they will be using different conventions, in this case exhibiting a global diversity effect.

We conclude this section with a final remark. We have to observe that in spite of the increasing interest in adaptive learning and evolution among game theorists, we are still laying down the basic elements of a theory. Indeed, if the main interest is just a few asymptotic properties or equilibrium selection, then the recent work we have discussed in this section is certainly more than satisfactory. But if we want to understand how agents learn and interact, the role that economic institutions and social norms play, the impact that different evolutionary environments have on achieving alternative social outcomes, then the theory is still in an early stage, and much work is still to be done.

6.4. THE FORMATION OF OPINIONS

There are cases in which asymmetric aggregate behaviour arises from the interaction between identical individuals, each of whom acts in a simple way. The behaviour of the group as a whole cannot be inferred from analyzing one of the identical individuals in isolation, and some sort of *herding behaviour* can be observed. There is a nice example by Becker (1991) about two apparently equivalent restaurants on either side of a street, and yet a large majority of people choose one rather than the other, just because of imitative behaviour, even though this behaviour involves waiting in line for a long time.

Models of 'mimetic behaviour', explained by the introduction of imitation, and processes that involve 'contagion', 'mimicking' or 'herding' have been thoroughly studied in the literature. The 'beauty contest' example, which was suggested by Keynes to explain how investors in asset markets often behave, is certainly a very famous example and is often quoted within this class of models.

One explanation offered in the literature is based on informational asymmetries. In Scharfstein and Stein (1990) the 'recruitment' follows from persuasion according to an agency problem: agents get rewards for convincing a principal that they are right. The idea is that, under certain circumstances, managers simply mimic the investment decisions of other managers, ignoring substantive private information. This behaviour is justified by reputational concerns; that is, it is a consequence of rational attempts by managers to enhance their reputations as decision-makers. This kind of principal–agent problem is especially studied in the context of asset markets. Another way of 'recruitment' follows from the fact that the choice made by the first agent may lead, through externality, to a second agent concurring in that choice. The herd externality can be based on strong complementarities. We discussed an example of this case in Chapter 4, when network externalities are present. Topol (1990) used this insight to provide an explanation of the observed excess volatility in asset markets: he develops a model in which agents obtain information held by other agents, and this also produces an epidemic type of effect. Other explanations of clustering behaviour are based on the analysis of how private information can cause individuals to coordinate on the actions of others. In most examples, there is no obvious principal–agent problem, but 'herd behaviour' comes from the fact that everyone is doing what everyone else is doing, even when their private information suggests doing something quite different. Banerjee (1993) considers the case where information transmission takes place in such a way that the recipient does not quite know whether or not to believe the information, and the probability that someone receives the information depends on how many people already have it. He calls these information transmission processes 'rumours'. More specifically, he considers an investment project with returns known only to a few people, who have to incur a cost which is private information. Agents receive only the information that someone else has invested, but are not told whether the investor knew the return or was just acting on the basis of the observation of others. The main result is that a positive fraction of those who observe the 'rumour' does not invest, which implies that a 'rumour' cannot mislead everybody. Orléan (1990) considers a model where bubbles in financial markets arise from what he calls 'mimetic contagion', and Welch (1992) studies the case where later potential investors can learn from the purchasing decisions of earlier investors when public offering of stocks are sold sequentially.

Notwithstanding the different ways of 'recruitment', these models have some common characteristics. First, there are agents who have to choose between different options on the basis of different tastes, expectations, beliefs, etc. and recruit other agents to their particular choice according to the different ways noted above. Second, these models are dynamic and switching of behaviour within a given population can be obtained: the system stays in one regime for some time before switching to another. The important element here is that the evolution of quite complicated dynamics follows from rather simple individual behaviour.

Let us make this issue more precise by means of a couple of examples. The first example is from Kirman (1993), about the evolution of two opinions over time in a population. The basic idea is stimulated by the observed behaviour of ants who, when faced with two apparently equivalent food sources, concentrate largely on one and then on the other. The feedback involved can be a higher probability of meeting a successful forager from the food source that is currently most frequented. Using a simple stochastic model developed jointly with Föllmer it is shown that provided there is a minimal amount of 'noise' in the system the proportion of ants feeding at each source will stay close to 1 or to 0 for a long time and then switch to the other extreme. Thus, in a symmetric situation with *a priori* symmetric agents, aggregate behaviour displays violent stochastic swings. Indeed, it can be shown that the distribution of the proportion of ants at the first source, for sufficiently large populations, becomes a symmetric beta distribution and for appropriate assumptions on the parameters of the model the distribution will be concentrated in the tails. Notice that the appropriate equilibrium notion here is a limit distribution of the underlying stochastic process. This is not a situation with multiple equilibria, in the usual sense, since every state is always revisited, and there is no convergence to any particular state.

A similar approach is in Agliardi and Bebbington (1994), where we consider the possibility of switching between two options within a given population. The idea of recruitment or contagion derives from the presence of externalities not necessarily of the informational type, and there is imprecise information about the other agents' choices. We find that the system lingers at prevalence of one option with intermittent transitions to prevalence of the other, using certain approximation results in the theory of population processes that allow us to represent the actions of an agent by a random process in order to draw inferences about the aggregate behaviour of the system, which will be almost deterministic. Our results are close to those obtained with evolutionary game theory, about equilibria selection under perpetual randomness, although our model does not apply evolutionary game theory.

It should be observed that the type of interactions we considered in this section do not depend on specifying any proximity of agents; that is, those who are more likely to meet with one another. This approach can be extended to study the modification of opinions when a neighbourhood structure, or a communication network, are modelled explicitly. This issue, which will be tackled again in the next section, has been raised by David (1988a, 1988b) through a witty example that we reproduce here. It is the famous 'snow-shovelling problem', which deals with coordination of behaviours, but can be reinterpreted in terms of diffusion of opinions. There is a city block lined with shops, and there is a snow-storm in progress. The pavement in front of each shop can be kept passable if the shopkeeper goes out from time to time and shovels the snow off. A typical shopkeeper rightly believes there will be a net benefit from shovelling his own bit of sidewalk only if the pavement outside at least one of the adjacent shops is being kept passable. Thus the rule of behaviour he will adopt is the following: he will keep his sidewalk clear if the two adjacent sidewalks are clear, while he will not do it if they are piled with snow; if one is clear and the other is not, he will continue a policy of shovelling with probability p. The question is: what can we expect to happen on this block as the storm goes on? It turns out that the evolution of each shopkeeper's behaviour follows a first-order Markov chain, and the collective behaviour of all the shopkeepers on the block can be viewed as a stochastic process formed from additively interacting Markov processes. Two absorbing states emerge: either total absence of collaboration (snow accumulates), or complete cooperation (snow is shovelled). Such an example is a particular case of the Ising model, where the neighbourhood structure of the system and local interactions matters for the study of the evolution of collective behaviour.

6.5. DYNAMIC MODELS OF LOCAL INTERACTIONS

Many of the recent contributions discussed above are also crucial in the literature on learning. Agents are assumed to use 'rules of thumb' or 'learning rules' when they decide how to move the next round of a sequence of games. A learning rule is just an arbitrary map from the past history of play, or some subset of it, into what to do next, and in many cases it is based on some statistic of how the last round was played. The central question in this literature is the limit configuration of play. If the learning rules which agents use have finite memory it is easy to show that the entire dynamical system can be viewed as a finite Markov chain, and supposing that agents can deviate from the behaviour prescribed by the learning rule because of 'mistakes' or 'noise', then, by standard results, the Markov chain describing the behaviour of the system will display a unique ergodic distribution, which represents the limit configuration of play and which is parametrized by the constant probability of mistakes. The equilibrium selection results can eventually be obtained as the 'noise' vanishes.

Of course, learning becomes much more complicated when it is not merely adaptive as it is in the interpretation of the models above, but, for example, agents try to anticipate the value of a variable, or form expectations; moreover, different agents may have different beliefs or different rules of learning (Blume and Easley, 1992; Easley and Kiefer, 1988). The interplay between the formation of beliefs and the dynamics of the system may become very intricate indeed.

Much of the literature has considered systems in which the learning rules that agents use are based on some statistic of the previous history of play of all agents in the system. There are few exceptions (Allen, 1982a, 1982b; Blume, 1991; Durlauf, 1989; Ellison, 1993; Ellison and Fudenberg, 1993) dealing with a class of systems in which agents learn from their neighbours only. The local nature of the learning interaction can be interpreted as a version of limited rationality, in the sense that agents are supposed to be informed only about the actions of their immediate neighbours, together with an assumption of costly information gathering activity. Most of these papers deal with dynamic models of local interactions and consider coordination problems.

Focusing on local interactions yields important analytical consequences. For example, it has been shown by Young (1993) that in a model of adaptive learning where interaction is not local, even in the absence of noise, convergence can be obtained for a large class of games with strategic complementarities. However, when interaction is local, convergence without noise may not obtain even in the simplest cases. Local interaction may yield stationary solutions of the system that are radically different from the stationary solutions of the non-local analogue of that system. This comes from the fact that in models of local interactions the dynamics are dependent on the locations of the agents using given strategies in addition to the aggregate frequencies. Ellison (1993) emphasizes the importance of local interaction as opposed to global uniform interaction in coordination games to show that, in certain circumstances, local interaction produces a surprisingly regular aggregate situation surprisingly rapidly.

Let us recall here the example in Ellison (1993). He considers a two by two coordination game like the one we represented in section 6.2, with $a > d$, and compares the situation in which all of N players are matched with uniform probability with the situation in which players are spatially distributed around a circle, so that each player can be matched only with their $2k$ immediate neighbours. In both cases, with no noise, there are two steady states (a state is the number of people playing s_1), that is, 0 and 1. However, if we look at local interactions and suppose that players can be matched with any of their nearest eight neighbours and, for example, let the payoffs be such that each player has s_1 as his best response whenever at least three of his eight neighbours play s_1, then it is apparent that players will choose s_1 if at least three of these neighbours did so in the previous period. The point here is that if there is a small cluster of players playing s_1 it will rapidly expand and take over the whole population. Indeed, suppose that the period t state is $(s_1, s_1, s_1, s_1, s_2, \ldots s_2)$ so that players 1 through 4 played s_1. Players 1 through 6 and players N and $N - 1$ all have at least three neighbours playing s_1. Those eight players will play s_1 in period $t + 1$. In period $t + 2$ players $N - 2, N - 3, 7$ and 8 will switch to playing s_1. Eventually, the state with s_1 for all players is reached. Once noise is introduced, then it is sufficient that four adjacent players switch to s_1 for the whole system to drift towards s_1. In the uniform matching model $(N - 1)/3$ simultaneous mutations would be necessary to shift from all s_2 to the basin of attraction of s_1; that is, the rate of convergence is slower in the model with uniform matching than in the case of local matching. One can therefore conclude that local interaction produces a surprisingly rapid convergence to a regular aggregate situation.

A typical model in which there is local interaction and in which the dynamic evolution of the aggregate behaviour is analyzed is that of Blume (1993). The assumption is that players, who are located at the vertices of an infinite connected graph, interact directly with a finite set of neighbours. No player interacts directly with everybody, but any two players indirectly interact through a finite chain of direct interactions. Each agent can be thought of as adopting a strategy and then receiving a payoff depending on the strategies adopted by his neighbours. Stochastic strategy revision processes are introduced, wherein each player revises his strategic choice in response to the play of his neighbours. Such stochastic strategy revision processes are defined as continuous-time Markov processes. Without entering into the details of the model, one of the questions here is to look at the limit behaviour of this process. It is found that if agents are very sensitive to the behaviour of their opponents, then the process may settle down to any one of a number of equilibrium configurations. On the contrary, when players are very unresponsive to payoff differences, the process is ergodic; that is, there is an invariant measure which describes the limit behaviour of the process. The crucial element in this analysis is how responsive is the probability of the choice of a strategy to that of the neighbours or, more precisely, to the increase in payoff that can be obtained by changing strategy, given the choice of the neighbours. Moreover, it is shown that even when Nash configurations exist, that is configurations in which every agent chooses the best response strategy, there is no simple connection between Nash configurations and equilibrium on the lattice.

The increasing interest in dynamic models of local interactions in recent years originates from the view that the local structure is recognized to be important to model the global properties of an economic system. The idea is that agents are limited to a set of neighbours with whom they interact (for example, agents may change their expectations as a function of the expectations of the others with whom they are in contact; they may be able to trade only with certain others; agents may communicate only with, or obtain information only from, a subset of the others, etc.) and therefore changes will not affect all agents simultaneously but rather diffuse across the economy. As Kirman (1996) has stressed, within such framework a notion of proximity and a 'neighbourhood structure' have to be appropriately defined: they may well be specified in terms of geographical distance, closeness in characteristics, or probability of interaction. In any case, the way in which diffusion of changes will occur and the speed with which it happens will depend crucially on the nature of the neighbourhood structure. Typically agents are thought of as being placed on a lattice and interacting with their neighbours. In this case, one is interested to know whether clusters with certain behaviour or characteristics may form.

Some interesting results in the literature about local interactions follow from the application of a branch of probability theory originally developed to characterize interacting particle systems. As we said in Chapter 2, the utilization of such mathematical tools to study social science questions is a fairly recent phenomenon. In particular, in the context of this section we wish to mention a few papers dealing with interdependent, or interacting, Markov processes. Allen (1982b) employed such tools to study technological diffusion under uncertainty of an innovation having externalities among users, for any arbitrary pattern of stochastic interactions among agents. Another example is Durlauf (1989), who studied an economy on a square integer lattice characterized by increasing returns to scale and localized trading among agents indexed by time and space. The model generates strong persistence in aggregate time series of output if the strength of local externalities at each production site is sufficiently high. Indeed, if such strength is high enough, that is, it reaches a critical level, then nonergodic time series emerge. Notice that this model requires some exogenous 'tuning' parameter to be increased to a critical level in order to generate the above-mentioned results about strong persistence and non-ergodicity.

In section 6.6, we shall discuss a model in which the kind of criticality is endogenous instead, not exogenous, and is of the 'self-organized' type.

6.6. MORPHOGENESIS OF AN INSTITUTION

Social institutions are predominantly concerned with solving social coordination problems. And in fact much of the analysis of how institutions emerge and change over time has been developed within a large class of games, namely coordination and common interest games, which are typically characterized by a multiplicity of equilibria. Most models discussed in the previous sections deal with this class of games.

Institutions, however, are not concerned only with solving social coordination problems. The class of institutions is indeed much broader than the class of social conventions. In many cases of economic interest, anti-coordination is more relevant. For instance, a system of property rights defines a regularity in behaviour that is socially agreed to. Yet this institution is not in equilibrium because each agent has an incentive to 'steal' from others. Another example of anti-coordination is technological competition modelled by innovation games.

In this section we study the morphogenesis of an institution in the anti-coordination case. Therefore, in our model imitative behaviour comes from 'strategic substitutability' and not from 'strategic complementarity' as it is, for example, in the models that involve 'herd behaviour', 'rumours', 'mimetic contagion' we discussed in section 6.4. To study morphogenesis, that is, the space–time pattern of the evolution of the players' actions, we consider local social interactions. We study a lattice game in which some degree of stability is reached over time after agents have tuned their actions to the moves of their neighbour agents. As we said in section 6.5, focusing on local interactions may yield interesting analytical consequences. Our main result here is that the structure we obtain has characteristics of 'self-organized criticality' (see Chapter 2, section 2.6). After a transient period, the system self-organizes into a configuration which is compatible with a high degree of differentiation among different sites, and generates power laws for the behaviour of objects such as spatial correlation functions, distribution of sizes of activity.

Notice that with the exception of Bak, Chen, Scheinkman and Woodford (1993) there are no papers, to the best of our knowledge, applying the model of self-organized criticality to economic problems. Their model, however, differ from ours because we consider a different lattice structure, a different specification of the random shock and a different source of local interaction. The purpose of this section is also to suggest a morphogenetic model within a field which has mainly concentrated on the study of asymptotic properties and equilibrium selection. The model is presented in section 6.6.1, while section 6.6.2 contains the main simulation results. Section 6.6.3 concludes with a few remarks and possible extensions.

6.6.1. The Model

Consider N agents arrayed on a one-dimensional circular lattice at a unitary discrete distance, where the agents' indices i denote locations. Neighbours of i are denoted by indices $i - 1$ and $i + 1$. The circular lattice implies that the left neighbour of agent 0 is agent $N - 1$ and the right neighbour of agent $N - 1$ is agent 0. Each agent has a choice of two possible actions: $\{0, 1\}$, and choices are irreversible; that is, switching is not allowed. We assume that the payoffs to agent i are such that they depend on i's action and the actions of neighbours i-1 and $i + 1$ only. This assumption is motivated by principles of bounded rationality: players are supposed to be informed only about the strategy choice of their immediate neighbours. This implies that there will be 2^3 combinations of actions. Table 6.1 specifies i's payoffs for an anti-coordination game:

Table 6.1   Payoffs for an anti-coordination game

$i-1$	i	$i+1$	i's payoff
0	1	0	2
0	1	1	1
1	1	0	1
1	1	1	−1
0	0	0	0
0	0	1	0
1	0	0	0
1	0	1	0

The choice of action 0 yields payoff 0. If agent i chooses action 1 and there is no competition by the two neighbours, then i's payoff is 2, while if there is just one competitor i's payoff is 1. In the case of competition by both neighbours agent i loses 1. The game can be interpreted in terms of technological competition where action 1 corresponds to adoption of an innovation, entry in a market which reduces the equilibrium price, diffusion of new ideas and scientific knowledge, etc. where 'strategic substitutability' is local.

In what follows we consider a dynamic formulation. The dynamics of this economic system are described as a spatio–temporal stochastic process according to the following rules.

Each i is subject to the realization of a random variable μ uniformly distributed in [0, 1]. The i^* with the highest realization chooses action 1. In this framework receiving the highest shock means that the agent, randomly selected, has had the most successful idea, 'mutation', from which a superior technology, a piece of knowledge, a new pricing policy stem. If we start from an initial condition characterized by all 0s for all agents and therefore by 0 payoffs for all agents, this implies that agent i^* will receive a payoff equal to 2, while the others continue to earn 0. In what follows we assume that agents consider their own cumulative payoffs; that is, they sum up their one-period payoff over time. The distribution of payoffs represents the distribution of property rights, and we are interested in asking how property rights do evolve. The payoffs are assumed to be locally observable by the two neighbours $i^* - 1$ and $i^* + 1$ who will adopt the following 'learning rule': if one of their neighbour's cumulative payoff is ≥ 2 than their own, then they will find it profitable to imitate that neighbour's action. Otherwise, they will stick with the action they did in the past. Reorganization in the payoff levels occurs as from Table 6.1. For example, if at the end of the reorganization period only $i^* - 1$ and $i^* + 1$ are imitators, they will get a payoff equal to 1 each, while i^* will get -1 as a result of competition, with cumulative payoffs equal to 1 for all of them (see Table 6.2).

Obviously, the 'learning rule' acts as a crucial element in the process of transmission in this system: through the chain of neighbours the effects of local externalities may spread along long distances too, until reorganization in the payoff levels stops.

At the end of the reorganization period we have a set of agents which have increased their level of payoffs while the complement of this set has not registered any change. Then we assume that new random noise $\mu'\epsilon[0, 1]$ is assigned only to all adjusted sites. This implies that if the vector of random shocks in the first period was $\mu = \{\mu_i$ for

Table 6.2   Payoffs at the end of the reorganization period

Actions	Payoffs
0 0 0 0 0 0 1 0	0 0 0 0 0 0 2 0
0 0 0 0 0 1 1 1	0 0 0 0 0 1 −1 1
	0 0 0 0 0 1 1 1

$i = 1, 2 \ldots N$}, in the following period the new random vector μ' will have new components μ_i' again uniform in [0, 1] only for the sites which have changed action, while the other components remain unchanged. Such an assumption seems to be plausible, given that agents who did not change their action will be facing the same decision problem as before and will maintain their previous period shock, while agents who did change their action in the previous period may be exposed to a new shock because of the change in environment conditions. Once the new vector of shocks is derived, the process is repeated choosing the site which has the new highest shock and starting a new round of reorganization, assigning payoffs as from Table 6.1.

Notice that in this setting the probability distribution of the random shock changes with time. The substitution of the maximal random shock and of all the other shocks of the sites which changed action with new random realizations, while keeping the other components unchanged, modifies the probability distribution for each site of being selected as the site with the new maximal random shock as a function of the history of previous realizations of the shocks. The features of the random mechanism are such that, at the beginning subsequent events are quite uncorrelated in space, but after a transient period the distribution of the maximal shocks becomes stationary and events become correlated. It can be shown that for any initial condition the system will reach a state where the spatial distribution of the subsequent sites with maximal shocks can be described by a power law distribution. We found this result through simulations and obtained that the probability of the spatial distance of two subsequent sites with maximal shocks scales as a power law with exponent equal to 2.25. Observe that a power law is expected within a model of self-organized criticality.

6.6.2. Some Simulations Results

Our study of the statistical properties of this model is simplified by the observation that it is formally identical to a 'sand pile' model exhibiting self-organized criticality. The theory of self-organized criticality has been discussed extensively in Chapter 2, section 2.6, and therefore we shall present here only the results of numerical simulations of our model.

First, in Figure 6.1 we have obtained the surface representing the distribution of cumulative payoffs for a system consisting of 65 players after 10100 runs of the basic anti-coordination game evolving according to the rules of section 6.6.1. Figure 6.1 represents the snapshot of a time–space stochastic process which starts with no asymmetries among players and, after a transient period, generates a highly asymmetric distribution of the payoffs in space. What is particularly interesting is the endogenous emergence of localized clusters of successful players, intermitted by less successful ones. Such configuration, which is characterized by a high degree of differentiation among different sites, has a straightforward interpretation, given what we said in section 6.6.1: it is the market configuration resulting from the processes of diffusion of knowledge, technological competition, pricing policies, etc. Moreover, both an accurate analysis of the surface and the study of the standard deviation of the cumulative payoffs reached in the different sites as a function of the system size (Figure 6.2), show the presence of fractal characteristics and self-affinity. Loosely speaking, this means that magnifying a particular subregion of the total space, the chosen part of the surface will reproduce the same geometrical features of the entire surface. We discussed the concept of self-similarity in Chapter 2, section 2.5. Self-affinity is a generalization of self-similarity. More specifically, an affine transformation transforms a point

$$x = (x_1, x_2, \ldots x_n)$$

into new points

$$x' = (r_1 x_1, r_2 x_2, \ldots r_n x_n)$$

where the scaling ratios $r_1, r_2, \ldots r_n$ are not all equal. A set S is statistically self-affine when S is the union of N non-overlapping subsets each of which is scaled down by r from the original and is identical in all statistical features to the set obtained from S by the affine transformation defined by r. In particular, a transformation that scales time and distance by different factors is called self-affine and curves that reproduce themselves in some sense under an affine transformation are called self-affine. One of these features is, for example, the *roughness of the surface*, expressed by means of the standard deviation of the cumulative payoffs among sites. The roughness increases with the number of players, following a *power law*, which means that the logarithmic transformation of the standard deviation increases linearly with the logarithm of the number of players, with a coefficient equal to 0.73. This is represented in Figure 6.2; the standard deviation has been calculated starting from the cumulative payoffs for a number of players ranging from 50 to 1000 players expressed by:

$$\text{std}(N) = \sqrt{\frac{1}{N} \sum_{i=1}^{N} (\Pi_{i,t} - \tilde{\Pi}_t)^2}$$

where $\tilde{\Pi}_t = (\sum_{i=1}^{N} \Pi_{i,t})/N$ and $\Pi_{i,t}$ is the cumulative payoff of player i at time t.

Power law relations among variables are interpreted as signs of a self-organized critical state. This means that the dynamics of the spatio–temporal stochastic process, describing the evolution of cumulative payoffs in time and among sites, seems to converge towards a configuration which is continuously changing, but which preserves, unchanged, certain features, like its roughness on all space-scales. From the literature on self-organized criticality it is known that

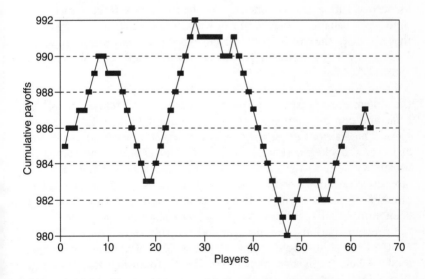

Figure 6.1 Cumulative payoffs distribution after 10100 runs of the game

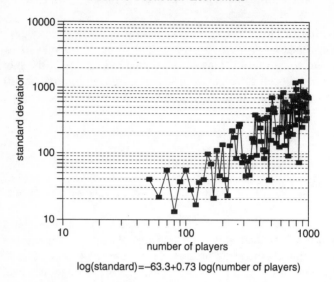

log(standard)=–63.3+0.73 log(number of players)

Figure 6.2   Standard deviation v. system size from 50 to 1000 players, 10000
            games

associated with a fractal dimension of the roughness in space there is a
time series behaviour the spectra of which reproduces the features of a
flicker noise, that is, a noise which expresses a superimposition of
signals at all the different frequencies (Bak, Tang and Wiesenfeld,
1988).

From Figure 6.3 we can analyze the typical aggregate variability in
the system at each period for 64 players after 10100 repetitions of the
basic anti-coordination game evolving according to the rules in section
6.6.1. The distribution of the changes in payoffs indeed describes the
aggregate shock generated by the individual choices. The aggregate
variability, that is, the numerosity of the sites which change actions,
remains constant over time, with a characteristic size of 4.32. The
number of players which change actions, and therefore register a
change in payoffs, defines the *size of an avalanche*, and depends on
the previous period configuration and the shocks realization. Figure
6.3 then represents the distribution of the sizes of avalanches for this
model, where the mean avalanche size is 4.32; following Bak, Tang and
Wiesenfeld (1988) one can show that a power law appears when
calculating the fraction of sites changing action as a function of time.

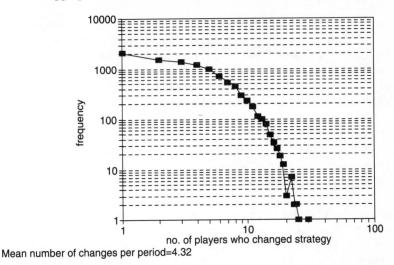

Mean number of changes per period=4.32

Figure 6.3   Distribution of strategy changes after 10100 runs with 64 players

6.6.3. Final Remarks

By explicitly recognizing the role of local structure on the global properties of an economic system, a rich class of models can be developed. A great deal of global regularity can emerge from these models. The approach and model of morphogenesis outlined above, although simplified, suggests a potentially fruitful direction where research could be addressed. The study of morphogenesis, that is, the spatio–temporal pattern of the evolution of the agents' action, seems to us important if we wish to understand how agents interact and learn in path-dependent systems, and how economic institutions and social norms evolve. Our model is just one step towards understanding the general phenomenon of the effect of local structure on global properties. A few remarks and extensions can be suggested.

We have focused on simple one-dimensional periodic lattices. An obvious generalization is to have a more complex lattice structure, for example, additional dimensions, randomly connected lattices, or lattices in which a few agents are connected to almost every other agents, etc. In our model agents are constrained to view only a small part of the history, say themselves and two neighbours, while an agent's information set might change by varying the neighbourhood size. If an agent is able to see the states of more neighbouring sites, then he might be able to better predict his neighbours' actions. In the analysis above, a crucial role is played by the 'learning rule' we have specified. Of course, the introduction of agents' expectations to predict neighbours' actions alters the structure of the model and may yield different results. Expectations formation is conditional on the information available to an agent, and thus strategies will be maps from the information to the set of actions.

An approach to the expectations problem is to treat the system as a set of coevolving agents. Agents would simultaneously evolve their strategies, perhaps employing some kind of learning or adaptive strategy. Kauffman (1992), for example, considers coevolution cast in the framework of game theory, namely Boolean games, and analyzes a system in which agents use a myopic strategy to alter their action. His oversimple model of coevolution consists of N agents to be coupled to K other agents (the so-called NK model), each of them choosing between two possible actions, 1 or 0, and taking into account the 2^{K+1} combinations of actions of the $K + 1$ agents, whose actions, 1 or 0, bear on a given agent's payoff. The payoff shows how well the agent does with that specific action when played in the context of the 1 or 0 actions of the K agents who affect it. Kauffman (1992) studies the endogenous dynamics of the coevolving system acted on by some form of selection and shows that, under certain conditions, the system may tend to a state of self-organized criticality. Such approach, however, has not yet been applied to economic problems.

Conclusion

There has been a steady development of dynamic analysis in economics in recent decades, both in theoretical work and in empirical implementations. Although the theoretical equations were frequently non-linear, the empirical methods often employed the tools of linear stochastic analysis; moreover, the economic theory underlying dynamical systems very often tended to emphasize amplitude-reducing behaviour, that is, negative feedbacks. In this book we have taken the perspective of positive feedback economies and have developed models where the observed distribution of economic activity might be determined by history.

It is not hard to find positive feedback elements in the real world. For example, it is evident that the presence and persistence of cyclical fluctuations of irregular timing and amplitude in the economy are not consistent with a view that an economy tends to return to equilibrium states after any disturbance. Similarly, different ethnic and class groups or economic regions within a country show irregular tendencies to converge, for example in terms of income, balanced by an equal and sometimes larger likelihood of divergence. Instead of stochastic steady states we often observe markets, such as financial markets, where volatility tends to vary greatly over time, with quiescent eras alternating with eras of rapid fluctuations.

Most examples we considered in this book deal with knowledge and technological choices. The analogy between evolution and technological progress has been almost a commonplace since the time of Darwin, and later on, among economists, since Schumpeter, but had in fact not led to much. In the last decade Nelson and Winter (1982) have made a much more elaborate attempt to create an evolutionary theory of innovation and imitation, typically with difference equations models in which rewards lead to expansion and failures to contraction. As we tried to show in this book, more definite and convincing results can be obtained from what we can call a 'complex systems approach'.

The challenge is now to develop further areas of research and applications within this approach. Some of them have already been indicated in this book, and many more can be thought of, especially within the broad topic concerning the coevolution of technologies, organizations and institutions and their macro implications. There are many more aspects of recent work in sciences which have potential analogies in economics and, in turn, economic phenomena and analysis may turn out to inspire new and different kinds of concepts in sciences. Selten (1991) trusts that 'eventually many theories of limited range will grow together and evolve into a comprehensive picture of economic behaviour'. We look forward to such systems-building.

Bibliography

AGLIARDI, E. 'Learning-by-Doing and the Emergence of Monopoly: a Note', *Economics Letters*, 34 (1990) 353–57

AGLIARDI, E. *Essays on the Dynamics of Allocation under Increasing Returns to Adoption and Path-Dependence*, Ph.D. dissertation, University of Cambridge (Cambridge, 1992a)

AGLIARDI, E. 'Learning-by-Doing and Implications on Market Structures', *Economic Notes*, 21 (1992b) 418–37

AGLIARDI, E. 'The Origin of Conventions', (Cambridge 1995) (mimeo)

AGLIARDI, E. and M.BEBBINGTON 'Self-reinforcing Mechanisms and Interactive Behaviour', *Economics Letters*, 46 (1994) 281–87

ALLEN, B. 'A Stochastic Interactive Model for the Diffusion of Information', *Journal of Mathematical Sociology*, 8 (1982a) 265–81

ALLEN, B. 'Some Stochastic Processes of Interdependent Demand and Technological Diffusion of an Innovation Exhibiting Externalities among Adopters', *International Economic Review*, 23 (1982b) 595–608

ANDERSON, P. W., K. ARROW and D. PINES (eds) *The Economy as an Evolving Complex System*, Santa Fe Institute Studies in the Sciences of Complexity (Reading MA: Addison-Wesley, 1988)

ARNOLD, V. I. *Catastrophe Theory*, 3d edn. (Berlin: Springer Verlag, 1992)

ARROW, K. J. 'The Economic Implications of Learning by Doing', *Review of Economic Studies*, 29 (1962) 155–73

ARROW, K. J. *The Limits of Organization* (New York: Norton, 1974)

ARROW, K. 'Economic History: a Necessary though not Sufficient Condition for an Economist', *American Economic Review, Papers and Proceedings*, 75 (1985) 320–23

ARROW, K. and F. HAHN *General Competitive Analysis* (New York: Holden-Day, 1971)

ARTHUR, W. B. 'Competing Technologies and Economic Prediction', *Options* (1984) 10–13

ARTHUR, W. B. 'Industry Location and the Importance of History', CEPR, Stanford University, Paper 84 (1986)

ARTHUR, W. B. 'Competing Technologies: An Overview', in G. Dosi, C. Freeman, R. Nelson, G. Silverberg. and L. Soete (eds) *Technical Change and Economic Theory*, (London: Pinter 1988a)

ARTHUR, W. B. 'Self-Reinforcing Mechanisms in Economics', in P. Anderson, K. Arrow and D. Pines (eds) *The Economy as an Evolving Complex System*, (Reading, MA: Addison-Wesley, 1988b)

ARTHUR, W. B. 'Competing Technologies, Increasing Returns and Lock-in by Historical Events', *Economic Journal*, 99 (1989) 116–31

ARTHUR, W. B. 'Positive Feedbacks in the Economy', *Scientific American*, 2 (1990) 80–85

ARTHUR, W. B. *Increasing Returns and Path Dependence in the Economy* (Ann Arbor, University of Michigan Press, 1994)

ARTHUR, W. B., Yu. M. ERMOLIEV and Yu. M. KANIOVSKI 'On Generalized Urn Schemes of the Polya Kind', *Kibernetika*, 19 (1983) 49–56. (English translation in Cybernetics, 19, 1983, 61–71)

ARTHUR, W. B., Yu. M. ERMOLIEV and Yu. M. KANIOVSKI 'Strong Laws for a Class of Path-Dependent Urn Processes', *Proceedings of the International Conference on Stochastic Optimization*, (Kiev 1984.) *Lecture Notes in Control and Information Sciences* 81, V. Arkin, A. Shiryayev and R. Wets (eds) (New York: Springer Verlag, 1985), 287–300

ARTHUR, W. B., Yu. M. ERMOLIEV and Yu. M. KANIOVSKI 'Non-linear Urn Processes: Asymptotic Behaviour and Applications', IIASA, Laxenburg, Working Paper 85–7 (1987a)

ARTHUR, W. B., Yu. M. ERMOLIEV and Yu. M. KANIOVSKI 'Path-Dependent Processes and the Emergence of Macrostructure', *European Journal of Operational Research*, 30 (1987b) 294–303

ATKINSON, A. B. and J. E. STIGLITZ 'A New View of Technological Change', *Economic Journal*, 79 (1969) 573–78

BAK, P. 'Self-organized Criticality', Scott Lectures, Cambridge (1994)

BAK, P. and K. CHEN 'Self-organized Criticality', *Scientific American*, 264 (1991) 46–51

BAK, P., K. CHEN, J. SCHEINKMAN and M. WOODFORD 'Aggregate Fluctuations from Independent Sectoral Shocks: Self-organized Criticality in a Model of Production and Inventory Dynamics', *Ricerche Economiche*, 47 (1993) 3–30

BAK, P., C. TANG and K. WEISENFELD 'Self-organized Criticality', *Physical Review* (A), 38 (1988) 364–78

BALASKO, Y. 'Economic Equilibrium and Catastrophe Theory: An Introduction', *Econometrica*, 46 (1978) 557–69

BANERJEE, A. V. 'A Simple Model of Herd Behaviour', *Quarterly Journal of Economics*, 107 (1992) 797–817

BANERJEE, A. V. 'The Economics of Rumours', *Review of Economic Studies*, 60 (1993) 309–27

BARNETT, W., J. GEWERKE and K. SHELL (eds) *Economic Complexity: Chaos, Sunspots, Bubbles and Nonlinearity.* Proceedings of the Fourth International Symposium in Economic Theory and Econometrics (Cambridge: Cambridge University Press, 1989)

BAUMOL, W. J. and J. BENHABIB 'Chaos: Significance, Mechanism, and Economic Applications', *Journal of Economic Perspectives*, 3 (1989) 77–107

BECKER, G. S. 'A Note on Restaurant Pricing and Other Examples of Social Influence on Price', *Journal of Political Economy*, 99 (1991) 1109–116

BELLMAN, R. 'A Problem in the Sequential Design of Experiments', *Sankhya*, 16 (1956), 221–9

BENHABIB, J. and K. NISHIMURA 'The Hopf Bifurcation and the Existence and Stability of Closed Orbits in Multisector Models of Optimal Economic Growth', *Journal of Economic Theory*, 21 (1979) 421–44

BERNHEIM, B. D. 'A Theory of Conformity', *Journal of Political Economy*, 102 (1994) 841–77.

BERRY, D. A. and B. FRISTEDT, *Bandit Problems: Sequential Allocation of Experiments* (London: Chapman & Hall, 1985)

BIKHCHANDANI, S., D. HIRSHLEIFER and I. WELCH 'A Theory of Fads, Fashion, Custom and Cultural Change as Informational Cascades', *Journal of Political Economy*, 100 (1992) 992–1026

BINMORE, K. G. 'Modelling Rational Players: I', *Economics and Philosophy*, 3 (1987) 179–214

BINMORE, K. G. 'Modelling Rational Players: II', *Economics and Philosophy*, 4 (1988) 9–55

BLUM, G. R. and M. BRENNAN 'On the strong law of large numbers for dependent random variables', *Israel Journal of Mathematics*, 3, (37) (1980), 241–5

BLUME, L. and D. EASLEY 'Evolution and Market Behaviour', *Journal of Economic Theory*, 58 (1992) 9–40

BLUME, L. 'The Statistical Mechanics of Strategic Interaction', *Games and Economic Behaviour*, 5 (1993), 387–424

BLUME, L. and D. EASLEY 'Economic Natural Selection', *Economics Letters*, 42 (1993) 281–89

BOLDRIN, M. and M. WOODFORD 'Equilibrium Models Displaying Endogeneous Fluctuations and Chaos: A Survey', *Journal of Monetary Economics*, 25 (1990) 189–223

BONANNO, G. 'Monopoly Equilibria and Catastrophe Theory', *Australian Economic Papers*, 5 (1987) 197–215

BOYD, R. and P. J. RICHERSON 'Rationality, Imitation , and Tradition', in R. H. Day and P. Chen (eds) *Non-linear Dynamics and Evolutionary Economics* (Oxford: Oxford University Press, 1993)

BROCK, W. A. 'Chaos and Complexity in Economic and Financial Science', in G. von Fustenberg (ed.) *Acting under Uncertainty: Multidisciplinary Conceptions* (Boston: Kluwer Academic Publishing, 1990)

BROCK, W.A. 'Understanding Macroeconomic Time Series Using Complex Systems Theory', *Structural Change and Economic Dynamics*, 2 (1991) 119–41

BROCK, W. A. and A. G. MALLIARIS *Differential Equations, Stability and Chaos in Dynamic Economics* (New York: North Holland, 1989)

CANNING, D. 'Average Behaviour in Learning Models', *Journal of Economic Theory*, 57 (1992) 442–72

CARLSSON, H. and E. van DAMME 'Global Games and Equilibrium Selection', *Econometrica*, 61 (1993a) 989–1026

CARLSSON, H. and E. van DAMME 'Equilibrium Selection in Stag Hunt Games', in K. Binmore, A. Kirman and P. Tani (eds) *Frontiers of Game Theory* (Cambridge, MA: MIT Press, 1993b)

CHAMLEY, C. and D. GALE 'Information Revelation and Strategic Delay in a Model of Investment', *Econometrica*, 62 (1994) 1065–85

COWAN, R. 'Nuclear Power Reactors: a Study in Technological Lock-in', *Journal of Economic History*, (1990) 541–67

COWAN, R. 'Tortoises and Hares: Choice among Technologies of unknown Merit', *Economic Journal*, 101 (1991) 801–13

CRAWFORD, V. P. 'An "Evolutionary" Interpretation of van Huyck, Battalio and Beil's Experimental Results on Coordination', Games and Economic Behaviour, *Games and Economic Behaviour*, 3 (1991) 25–59

CUGNO, F. and L. MONTRUCCHIO 'Disequilibrium Dynamics in a Multidimensional Macroeconomic Model: A Bifurcation Approach', *Ricerche Economiche*, 37 (1983) 3–21

DASGUPTA, P. 'The Economic Theory of Technology Policy: An Introduction', in P. Dasgupta and P. Stoneman (eds) *Economic Policy and Technological Performance* (Cambridge: Cambridge University Press, 1987)

DASGUPTA, P. 'Patents, Priority and Imitation or, the Economics of Races and Waiting Games', *Economic Journal*, 98 (1988) 66–80

DASGUPTA, P. *An Enquiry into Well-Being and Destitution* (Oxford: Clarendon Press, 1993)

DASGUPTA, P. and P. DAVID 'Information Disclosure and the Economics of Science and Technology', in G. Feiwel (ed.) *Issues in Contemporary Microeconomics and Welfare* (London: Macmillan, 1987)

DASGUPTA, P. and J. STIGLITZ 'Learning-by-Doing, Market Structure and Industrial and Trade Policies', *Oxford Economic Papers*, 40 (1988b) 246–68

DAVID, P. *Technical Choice Innovation and Economic Growth* (Cambridge: Cambridge University Press, 1975)

DAVID, P. 'Clio and the Economics of QWERTY', *American Economic Review*, 75 (1985) 332–37

DAVID, P. 'Some New Standards for the Economics of Standardization in the Information Age', in P. Dasgupta and P. Stoneman (eds) *Economic Policy and Technological Performance* (Cambridge: Cambridge University Press, 1987)

DAVID, P. 'Path-Dependence: Putting the Past into the Future of Economics', IMSSS, *Technical Report*, 533, Stanford University (1988a)

DAVID, P. 'The Future of Path-Dependent Equilibrium Economics', CEPR, Stanford University (1988b)

DAVID, P. 'Why are Institutions the "Carriers of History"?', *Structural Change and Economic Dynamics*, 5 (1994), 205–220

DAVID, P. and D. FORAY 'Dynamics of Competitive Technology Diffusion through Local Network Structures: the Case of EDI Documents Standards' in E. Leysendorff (ed.) *New Developments in Technology Studies*, (Amsterdam: Elsevier Scientific, 1994)

DAY, R. H. *Complex Economic Dynamics*, vol. I (Cambridge, MA: MIT Press, 1993)

DE GROOT, M. H. *Optimal Statistical Decisions* (New York: McGraw-Hill, 1970)

DHAR, D. and R. RAMASWAMY 'Exactly Solved Models of Self-organized Criticality', *Physical Review Letters*, 63, 16 (1989) 1659–62

DIXIT, A. 'Investment and Hysteresis', *Journal of Economic Perspectives*, 6 (1992a) 107–32

DIXIT, A. 'Irreversible Investment with Uncertainty and Scale Economies', mimeo, Princeton University (1992b)

DIXIT, A. and R. S. PINDYCK, *Investment under Uncertainty* (Princeton: Princeton University Press, 1994)

DOSI, G., F. FREEMAN, R. NELSON, G. SILVERBERG and L. SOETE (eds) *Technical Change and Economic Theory* (London, Pinter 1988)

DOSI, G. and Yu. KANIOVSKI 'The Method of Generalized Urn Scheme in the Analysis of Technological and Economic Dynamics', mimeo, IIASA, Laxenburg (1993)

DURLAUF, S. N. 'Locally Interacting Systems, Coordination Failure, and the Behaviour of of Aggregate Activity', mimeo, Stanford University (1989)

DURLAUF, S. N. 'Non-ergodic Economic Growth', *Review of Economic Studies*, 60 (1993) 23–41

DURRETT, R. *Lecture Notes on Particle Systems and Percolation* (Monterey, California, Wadsworth and Brooks/Cole, 1988)

DYBVIG, P. H. and C. S. SPATT 'Adoption Externalities as Public Goods', *Journal of Public Economics*, 20 (1983) 231–47

EASLEY, D. and N. M. KIEFER 'Controlling a Stochastic Process with Unknown Parameters', *Econometrica*, 56 (1988) 1045–64

ELLISON, G. 'Learning, Local Interaction and Coordination *Econometrica*, 61 (1993) 1047–71

ELLISON, G. and D. FUDENBERG 'Rules of Thumb for Social Learning', *Journal of Political Economy*, 101 (1993) 612–43

FARRELL, J. and G. SALONER 'Standardization, Compatibility, and Innovation', *Rand Journal of Economics*, 16 (1985) 70–83

FARRELL, J. and G. SALONER 'Standardization and Variety', *Economics Letters*, 20 (1986a) 71–4

FARRELL, J. and G. SALONER 'Installed Base and Compatibility: Innovation, Product Preannouncements and Predation', *American Economic Review*, 76 (1986b) 940–55

FARRELL, J. and G. SALONER 'Competition, Compatibility and Standards: the Economics of Horses, Penguins and Lemmings', *Working Paper*, E-86–73, The Hoover Institution, Stanford University (1986c)

FARRELL, J. and C. SHAPIRO 'Dynamic Competition with Switching Costs', *Rand Journal of Economics*, 3 (1988) 123–37

FELLER, W. *An Introduction to Probability Theory*, vol. I (New York: Wiley, 1968)

FELLER, W. *An Introduction to Probability Theory*, vol. II (New York: Wiley, 1971)

FÖLLMER, H. 'Random Economies with Many Interacting Agents', *Journal of Mathematical Economics*, 1 (1974) 51–62

FOSTER, D. and P. YOUNG 'Stochastic Evolutionary Game Dynamics', *Theoretical Population Biology*, 38 (1990) 219–32

FRIEDMAN, D. 'Evolutionary Games in Economics', *Econometrica*, 59 (1991) 637–66

FUDENBERG, D. and J. TIROLE 'Learning-by-Doing and Market Performance', *Bell Journal of Economics*, 71 (1983) 522–530

FUDENBERG, D. and C. HARRIS 'Evolutionary Dynamics with Aggregate Shocks', *Journal of Economic Theory*, 57 (1992) 420–41

FUTIA, C.A. 'Invariant Distributions and the Limiting Behaviour of Markovian Economic Models, *Econometrica*, 50 (1982) 377–408

GHEMAWATT, P. and M. SPENCE 'Learning Curve Spillovers and Market Performance', *Quarterly Journal of Economics*, 32(1985) 839–52

GITTINS, J.C. 'Bandit Processes and Dynamic Allocation Indices', *Journal of the Royal Statistical Society B*, 41 (1979) 148–77

GOODWIN, R.M. *Essays in Economic Dynamics* (London: Macmillan, 1982)

GOLUBITSKY, M and D.J. SCHAEFFER *Singularities and Groups in Bifurcation Theory* (New York, Springer Verlag, 1985)

GOULD, S.J. and N. ELDREDGE 'Punctuated Equilibria: an Alternative to Phyletic Gradualism', in T.J.M. Schopf (ed.), *Models in Paleobiology* (San Francisco: Freeman Cooper & Co, 1972)

GOULD, S.J. and N. ELDREDGE 'Punctuated Equilibrium Comes of Age', *Nature*, 366 (1993) 223–7

GRANDMONT, J.M. (ed.) *Nonlinear Economic Dynamics* (New York: Academic Press, 1987)

GRANOVETTER, M. 'Threshold Models of Collective Behaviour', *American Journal of Sociology*, 7 (1978) 1420–43

GRANOVETTER, M. and R. SOONG 'Threshold Models of Interpersonal Effects in Consumer Demand', *Journal of Economic Behaviour and Organization*, 7 (1986) 83–99

GREIF, A. 'Cultural Beliefs and the Organization of Society: A Historical and Theoretical Reflection on Collectivist and Individualist Societies', *Journal of Political Economy*, 102 (1994) 912–50

GUCKENHEIMER, J. and P. HOLMES *Nonlinear Oscillations, Dynamical Systems and Bifurcations of Vector Fields* (New York: Springer Verlag, 1983)

GRIMMETT, G. *Percolation* (New York: Springer Verlag, 1989)

HABERMEIER, K.F. 'Competing Technologies, the Learning Curve and Rational Expectations', *European Economic Review*, 33 (1989) 1293–311

HAHN, F.H. 'Stability', in K.J. Arrow and M. Intriligator (eds) *Handbook of Mathematical Economics*, vol.II (Amsterdam: North-Holland, 1982)

HAHN, F.H. 'In Praise of Economic Theory', in F.H.Hahn (ed.) *Money, Growth and Stability* (Oxford: Basil Blackwell, 1985)

HAHN, F.H. 'Information Dynamics and Equilibrium', in F.H. Hahn (ed.) *The Economics of Missing Markets, Information and Games* (Oxford: Clarendon Press, 1989)

HAKEN, H. *Synergetics*, 3rd edn (New York: Springer Verlag, 1983)

HAKEN, H. 'Chaos and Order in Nature', in H. Haken (ed.) *Chaos and Order in Nature*, Proceedings of the International Symposium on Synergetics at Schloss Ehnau (Berlin: Springer Verlag, 1981)

HAKEN, H. *Information and Self-Organization* (Berlin: Springer Verlag, 1988)

HANSON, W.A. Bandwagon and Orphans: Dynamic Pricing of Competing Systems subject to Decreasing Costs, Ph.D. dissertation (Stanford University, 1985)

HARSANYI, J.C. and R. SELTEN *A General Theory of Equilibrium Selection in Games* (Cambridge, MA: MIT Press, 1988)

HEAL, G. 'Macrodynamics and Returns to Scale', *Economic Journal*, 96 (1986) 191–98

HELPMAN, E. and P. KRUGMAN *Market Structure and Foreign Trade* (Cambridge, MA: MIT Press, 1985)

HIRSHMAN, A. *The Strategy of Economic Development* (New Haven: Yale University Press, 1958)

JENSEN, R. 'Adoption and Diffusion of an Innovation of Uncertain Profitability', *Journal of Economic Theory*, 27 (1982) 182–93

KANDORI, M., G. J. MAILATH and R. ROB 'Learning, Mutation and Long Run Equilibria in Games', *Econometrica*, 61 (1993) 29–56

KATZ, M. L. and C. SHAPIRO 'Network Externalities, Competition and Compatibility', *American Economic Review*, 75 (1985) 424–40

KATZ, M. L. and C. SHAPIRO 'Technology Adoption in the Presence of Network Externalities', *Journal of Political Economy*, 94 (1986a) 822–41

KATZ, M. L. and C. SHAPIRO 'Product Compatibility Choice in a Market with Technological Progress', *Oxford Economic Papers*, 38 (1986b) 146–65

KATZ, M. L. and C. SHAPIRO 'Product Introduction with Network Externalities', *Journal of Industrial Economics*, 40 (1992) 55–83

KAUFFMAN, S. A. *The Origin of Order* (Oxford: Oxford University Press, 1992)

KEHOE, T. J. 'Multiplicity of Equilibria and Comparative Statics', *Quarterly Journal of Economics*, 100 (1985) 119–47

KELLY, F. P. *Reversibility and Stochastic Networks* (Chichester: Wiley, 1979)

KESTEN, H. *Percolation Theory for Mathematicians* (Boston: Birkhauser, 1982)

KESTEN, H. 'The Incipient Infinite Cluster in Two-dimensional Percolation', *Probability Theory and Related Fields*, 73 (1986) 369–94

KIM, Y. 'Adjustments, Evolution and Equilibrium Selection in Coordination Games', *Economic Theory Discussion Paper* 195, University of Cambridge (1993)

KINDERMANN, R. P. and J. L. SNELL 'On the Relation Between Markov Random Fields and Social Networks', *Journal of Mathematical Sociology*, 7 (1980) 1–13

KIRMAN, A. 'Communication in Markets', *Economics Letters*, 22 (1983) 101–7

KIRMAN, A. 'Epidemics of Opinion and Speculative Bubbles in Financial Markets' in M.Taylor (ed.) *Money and Financial Markets* (London: Macmillan, 1991)

KIRMAN, A. 'Ants, Rationality and Recruitment', *Quarterly Journal of Economics*, 2 (1993) 137–56

KIRMAN, A. 'Interaction and Markets', mimeo, GREQAM (1996)

KREPS, D. and M. SPENCE 'Modelling the Role of History in Industrial Organization and Competition', in G.R. Feiwel (ed.) *Issues in Contemporary Microeconomics and Welfare* (London: Macmillan, 1985)

KRUGMAN, P. R. *Rethinking International Trade* (Cambridge MA: MIT Press, 1990)

KRUGMAN, P.R. *The Self-Organizing Economy* (Oxford, Basil Blackwell, 1996)

KURZ, T.G. 'Strong Application Theorems for Density Dependent Markov Chains', *Stochastic Processes and Applications*, 6 (1978) 223–40

LEE IN HO, 'On the Convergence of Informational Cascades', *Journal of Economic Theory*, 61 (1993) 395–411

LESOURNE, J. *The Economics of Order and Disorder* (Oxford: Clarendon Press, 1992)

LIGGETT, T.M. *Interacting Particle Systems* (New York: Springer Verlag, 1985)

LUCAS, R. 'On the Mechanics of Economic Development', *Journal of Monetary Economics*, (1985) 3–42

LUCAS, R.E. and N.L. STOKEY *Recursive Methods in Economic Dynamics* (Cambridge, MA: Harvard University Press, 1989)

LUCCIO, F. and L. PAGLI (ed.) 'La Matematica della Complessita', *Le Scienze, Quaderni*, 67

MAILATH, G.J. 'Perpetual Randomness in Evolutionary Economics', *Economics Letters*, 42 (1993) 291–9

MATSUYAMA, K. 'Increasing Returns, Industrialization and Indeterminacy of Equilibrium, *Quarterly Journal of Economics*, 106 (1991) 617–650

MEDIO, A. and G. GALLO *Chaotic Dynamics: Theory and Applications to Economics* (Cambridge: Cambridge University Press, 1992)

MEHTA, A.'Real Sandpiles: Dilatancy, Hysteresis and Cooperative Dynamics', *Physica*, 186 (1992), 121–53

MEHTA, A. and G. BARKER 'The Self-organising Sand Pile', *New Scientist*, 6 (1991) 40–43

MOOKHERJEE, D. and D. RAY 'Learning-by-doing and Industry Market Structure: an Overview', in Dutta, B. *et al.* (eds) *Theoretical Themes in Development Economics* (Oxford: Oxford University Press, 1989)

MOOKHERJEE, D. and D. RAY 'On the Competitive Pressure Created by the Diffusion of Innovations', *Journal of Economic Theory*, 55 (1991) 124–47

MOWERY, D.C. and N. ROSENBERG *Technology and the Pursuit of Economic Growth* (Cambridge: Cambridge University Press, 1989)

MYRDAL, G. *Economic Theory and Underdeveloped Regions* (London: Duckworth, 1957)

NELSON, R. and S. WINTER *An Evolutionary Theory of Economic Change* (Cambridge MA: Harvard University Press, 1982)

NICOLIS, G. and I. PRIGOGINE *Self-Organization in Nonequilibrium Systems: from Dissipative Structures to Order Through Fluctuations* (New York: Wiley, 1976)

NICOLIS, G. and I. PRIGOGINE *Exploring Complexity* (New York: Freeman, 1989)

NORTH, D.C. *Institutional Structure and Institutional Change* (New York: Cambridge University Press, 1990)

ORLÉAN, A. 'Le Role des Influences Interpersonelles dans la Determination des Cours Boursiers', *Revue Economique*, V (1990) 839–68

PINDYCK, R.S. 'Irreversibility, Uncertainty and Investment', *Journal of Economic Literature*, 29 (1991) 1110–48

POSCH M. 'Learning in Games Modeled by Urn Schemes', London (1993) (mimeo)

POSTON, T. and I. STEWART *Catastrophe Theory and its Applications* (London: Pitman 1978)

PRIGOGINE, I. and I. STENGERS *Entre le Temps et l'Eternité* (Paris, Fayard, 1988)

ROHLFS, J. 'A Theory of Interdependent Demand for a Communication Service', *Bell Journal of Economics*, 5 (1974) 16–37

ROMER, P. 'Increasing Returns and Long-run Growth', *Journal of Political Economy*, 94 (1986) 1002–37

ROSENBERG, N. *Perspectives on Technology* (Cambridge: Cambridge University Press, 1976)

ROSENBERG, N. *Inside the Black Box: Technology and Economics* (Cambridge: Cambridge University Press, 1982)

ROSENBERG, N. 'Why do Firms do Basic Research (with their Own Money ?)', *Research Policy*, 12 (1990) 167–74

ROTHSCHILD, M. 'A Two Armed Bandit Theory of Market Pricing', *Journal of Economic Theory*, 9 (1974a) 185–202

ROTHSCHILD, M. 'Searching for the Lowest Price when the Distribution of Prices is Unknown', *Journal of Political Economy*, 82 (1974b) 689–711

RUELLE, D. *Elements of Differentiable Dynamics and Bifurcation Theory* (San Diego CA, Academic Press, Harcourt Brace Jovanovich, 1989a)

RUELLE, D. *Chaotic Evolution and Strange Attractors* (Cambridge: Cambridge University Press, 1989)

SAMUELSON, L. 'Recent Advances in Evolutionary Economics: Comments', *Economics Letters*, 42 (1993) 313–19

SATTINGER, D. H. 'Group Representation Theory and Branch Points of Nonlinear Functional Equations', *Siam Journal of Mathematical Analysis*, 8 (1977), 179–201

SATTINGER, D. H. 'Group Representation Theory, Bifurcation Theory and Pattern Formation', *Journal of Functional Analysis*, 28 (1978), 58–101

SATTINGER, D. H. 'Group Theoretic Methods in Bifurcation Theory', *Lecture Notes in Mathematics* n. 762 (Berlin: Springer Verlag, 1979)

SAUNDERS, P. T. *An Introduction to Catastrophe Theory* (Cambridge: Cambridge University Press, 1980)

SCHARFSTEIN, D. S. and J. C. STEIN, 'Herd Behaviour and Investment', *American Economic Review*, 80 (1990) 465–79

SCHELLING, T. *The Strategy of Conflict* (Cambridge MA: Harvard University Press, 1960)

SCHELLING, T. *Micromotives and Macrobehaviour* (New York: Norton, 1978)

SCHOTTER, A. *The Economic Theory of Social Institutions* (Cambridge: Cambridge University Press, 1981)

SCHUMPETER, J. A. *Capitalism, Socialism and Democracy* (New York: Harper, 1950)

SELTEN, R. 'Evolution, Learning and Economic Behaviour', *Games and Economic Behaviour*, 3 (1991) 3–24

SHESHINSKI, E. 'Tests of the Learning-by-doing Hypothesis, *Review of Economics and Statistics*, 49 (1967) 568–78

SOLOW, R. 'Economics: is Something Missing?', *American Economic Review*, 75 (1985) 320–37

SPENCE, M. 'The Learning Curve and Competition', *Bell Journal of Economics*, 12 (1981) 49–70

STANLEY, M., L. AMARED, S. BULDYREN, S. HAVIIN, H. LESCHHORN, P. MAASS, M. SALINGER and H. STANLEY 'Behaviour in the Growth of Companies', *Nature*, 379 (1996), 804–6

STEIN, D. L. (ed.) *Lectures in the Sciences of Complexity*, Santa Fe Institute Studies in the Sciences of Complexity, (Reading, MA: Addison Wesley, 1989)

STIGLITZ, J. E. 'Learning to Learn, Localized Learning and Technological Progress', in P. Dasgupta and P. Stoneman (eds) *Economic Policy and Technological Performance* (Cambridge: Cambridge University Press, 1987)

STOKEY, N. 'The Dynamics of Industrywide Learning', in W. P. Heller, R. M. Starr and D. A. Starrett (eds) *Equilibrium Analysis: Essays in Honour of K. J. Arrow*, vol.II (Cambridge: Cambridge University Press, 1986)

SUGDEN, R. *The Economics of Rights, Cooperation and Welfare* (Oxford: Basil Blackwell, 1986)

TOPOL, R. 'Bubbles and Volatility of Stock Prices', *Financial Market Group Discussion Paper Series*, 101 (London School of Economics, 1990)

Van HUYCK, J.C., R. C. BATTALIO and R. O. BEIL 'Tacit Coordination Games, Strategic Uncertainty and Coordination Failure', *American Economic Review*, 80 (1990) 234–48

WEIDLICH, W. 'The Use of Statistical Models in Sociology', *Collective Phenomena*, (1971) 51–9

WEIDLICH, W. 'Physics and Social Science – The Approach of Synergetics', *Physics Reports* 204 (1991) 1–163

WEIDLICH, W. and M. BRAUN 'The Master Equation Approach to Nonlinear Economic Processes', *Papers on Economics and Evolution*, ESGEE, n.9101 (1991)

WEIDLICH, W. and G. HAAG *Concepts and Models of a Quantitative Sociology* (Berlin: Springer Verlag, 1983)

WEISS, A. 'A New Technique for Analyzing Large Traffic Systems', *Advanced Applied Probability*, 18 (1986) 506–32

WELCH, I. 'Sequential Sales, Learning, and Cascades', *Journal of Finance*, 47 (1992) 695–732

WHITTLE, P. 'Arm-acquiring Bandits', *Annals of Probability,* 9 (1981), 284–91

WHITTLE, P. *Systems in Stochastic Equilibrium*, (Chichester: Wiley, 1986)

WHITTLE, P. 'Restless Bandits: Activity Allocation in a Changing World', *Applied Probability*, 9 (1988) 287–298

WITT, U. 'Path-Dependence in Institutional Change', *Papers on Economics and Evolution*, ESGEE, 9306 (1993)

WOODFORD, M. 'Imperfect Financial Intermediation and Complex Dynamics' in W. Barnett, J. Geweke and K.Shell (eds) *Economic Complexity: Chaos, Sunspots, Bubbles and Non-linearity* (Cambridge: Cambridge University Press, 1989)

YOUNG, A. 'Increasing Returns and Economic Progress', *Economic Journal*, 38 (1928) 527–42

YOUNG, H. P. 'The Evolution of Conventions', *Econometrica*, 61 (1993) 57–84

YOUNG, H. P. 'The Economics of Conventions', *Journal of Economic Perspectives*, 10 (1996) 105–22

YUNG-CHEN Lu, *Singularity Theory and an Introduction to Catastrophe Theory* (New York: Springer Verlag, 1976)

ZEEMAN, E. C. 'The Classification of Elementary Catastrophes of Codimension ≤ 5', in A. Dolb and B. Eckmann (eds) *Structural Stability, the Theory of Catastrophes and Applications in the Sciences* (New York: Springer-Verlag, 1976)

ZEEMAN, E. C. *Catastrophe Theory* (Reading, MA: Addison-Wesley, 1977)

Index